# JAMES BROOKS KINZER:
## An American Life

Edited and Annotated
by

Janet Kinzer
and
Margaret Kinzer Meyers

ISBN: 979-83493222-7-3

Sligo Creek Publishing
9039 Sligo Creek Parkway
Silver Spring, Maryland 20901
https://sligocreekpublishing.com

# CONTENTS

# INTRODUCTION

Late in life Dad began writing notes about his life, memories that were mostly about his young years growing up in central Pennsylvania and his service in World War II.

Dad began his memoirs and then began them again, and then again. So, we have combined three versions of his memories into one. Dad had a nice narrative flow, simple story telling, but he repeated himself in the three versions and some of the stories were - maddeningly - dropped midway or undeveloped. Sometimes the reader wants more information, but he didn't include it.

I think Dad wanted to share these parts of his life, the formative years, with his children and grandchildren so that we would know about our own roots, which are deeply embedded in a more rural and simpler America. And he wanted us to know how circumstances, especially the Great Depression and his service in World War II, transformed him and then shaped the lives of his children and grandchildren. We knew him as Dad and Granddad, he wants us to know him as Jimmy, Lieutenant Kinzer, and Jim.

With the 100th anniversary of his birth this summer, I thought I would revisit his memories and supplement them with stories he told us throughout the years, along with some genealogical information about Dad's family, and some of the photos in my possession, to provide additional context for Dad's recollections.

The American part of the Kinzer story goes back almost 300 years in America. "We," The Kinzers, arrived here in the early 1730s. Other parts of our family arrive in America even earlier than that - especially our English, Scots, and Dutch ancestors. Many were seeking religious freedom when they came here, decades before there was an America. That makes the story of Dad's family a stand-in for the story of many Americans.

# THE WILLIAMS AND MAUK FAMILIES
## OF ROARING SPRING

*Roaring Spring is a lovely small town, one we five Kinzer kids all remember fondly from our many road trips to Pennsylvania. The town itself dates back to the 1760s, but for the next century it was little more than an outpost and crossroads with a grist mill and a few homes.*

*The first paper mill opened in 1865. With new businesses making a real Main St, a new railroad line, and the Civil War over, Roaring Spring began to grow, attracting families from nearby rural areas, including the Kinzer and Williams families.*

*When we were kids visiting Dad's folks there was a sense of otherness in the town. We kids lived a modern, suburban life so Roaring Spring was a curiosity to us, with its narrow streets, curious-looking old houses right up at the curb, clotheslines, chained dogs, and lots of really, really old people in well-worn clothes and sturdy shoes. To us, it was quaint. The main attraction, besides our very loving grandparents, was the shady park centered around a spring, where there was also a bandstand, and a pond full of enormous goldfish. aged trout, and ducks. We always liked feeding them –bread or popcorn.*

In Roaring Spring we lived among my mother's people, the Williams family. This was a large and well-established family, settled around here before there was a town, and even before the Civil War. I knew three or four generations of the Williams family. They were religious people, devout and a little prim in that small-town way, and very proud of themselves.

My mother, Mary Lillian, was the youngest daughter in this big family, and much adored. I never talked with my mother about her family origins and background. She knew her own part of the family, of course, but she related nothing to me of their origins. It was as though the Williams family began with her grandfather, J.A.J. Williams, when he showed up in Roaring Spring just after the Civil War.

John Andrew Jackson Williams was part of the Third Great Awakening in the US, the third revival and expansion of Methodists and Baptists in the US. In 1866, J.A.J. Williams organized a revival meeting just outside Roaring Spring, attracting a large crowd and converting enough people to warrant a Methodist church in town. Before that, Roaring Spring was on a circuit where you might have a minister to lead your service once a month. This was an important development for the growing town.

I never met the Rev. J.A.J. Williams, my great-grandfather. He died long before I was born. Even so, John Andrew Jackson Williams was well-known in Roaring Spring and he was often mentioned in the course of family-talk. Like most young men in Pennsylvania he had served in the Union Army in the Civil War. But we were told he was a reluctant volunteer and joined the war late, realizing he couldn't sit this war out, even if he felt it was against his religion to kill. He was already a lay minister in the Methodist Church, when he joined. That was his calling, but he made his living as a skilled carpenter and then as a contractor and businessman.

I was told that when my family arrived in Roaring Spring it was little more than a crossroad with a few log cabins scattered around. Over the next decades, J.A.J Williams, with his sons, built many of the houses located on the oldest streets of the town. Many are still there today, so they did good work. Just look for a red brick house with an ornate porch that faces the street and built before 1900, and that's probably a J.A.J. Williams house. When I was a boy, whether driving or walking, my Williams relatives would always point out the houses J.A.J Williams and his sons had built.

As you can tell, the Methodist church anchored the Williams family. My Williams uncles were all named for Methodist Bishops! The church my family was so instrumental in building, Trinity United Methodist Church, is still in operation in the center of the oldest part of Roaring Spring. The current church is the second building. The Rev J.A.J. Williams oversaw the fund raising and construction of the first church, and then he did it all over again for the second, much larger church, built in stone, complete with a bell tower and stained glass windows. Something to be proud of.

The United Methodist church in its second iteration. If you look, there's a stained-glass window dedicated to J.A.J. Williams. This image is from a postcard commissioned by Lambert's Pharmacy, Roaring Spring, Glenn Williams, Dad's uncle, purchased this pharmacy in 1943.

In the new church there's also a baptismal font, central to any Christian church, donated by James Shane Williams, my grandfather, and dedicated to my grandmother, Annetta Mauk Williams, the mother of their 12 children.

The Williams family could just about fill a church on their own. J.A.J was married to Mary Jane Gilliland in 1854 and they had twelve children. She was from another well-settled area family. and both lived to celebrate a 50th wedding anniversary, not long after my Mother was born. Eight of their twelve children survived to attend the celebration along with their spouses, children and grandchildren. I was told by my Mother that they had about 150 descendants at that party.

I am proud that there have always been members of my family in our nation's wars. Our ancestor, David Gilliland, was a Revolutionary War soldier, guarding the frontier at Hollidaysburg, PA. At that time this area was on the edge of the Iroquois Nation, which sided with the English.

We then had two great-grandfathers on my mother's side who fought in the Civil War. J.A.J. Williams enlisted in 1864, when he was 31. In 1862, George W. Mauk was 30 when he became a 90-day enlistee. He fought at Antietam, one of the bloodiest battles fought in the Civil War. [We have included an appendix listing many of our ancestors who served; Dad was only aware of a few of these veterans.]

I had two Williams uncles who served in WWI: Uncle Byron Williams and Ed Williams. Both were wounded, Byron very seriously by shrapnel. It was touch and go for a long time. As his wounds healed, he had blood clots that pressed against his heart. When that happened the wounds would have to be reopened and cleaned. This happened several times, and he would be near death, until new treatments were developed.

I have seen a letter written to Annetta Mauk Williams by Byron's captain saying what a fine soldier he was. Byron visited the VA Hospital in Pittsburgh, and was stopped by a man who recognized him. He said, "I'm the soldier who found you on the battlefield and carried you to the field hospital!"

James Shane Williams, my grandfather, was the "lead Accountant" at the Roaring Spring Blank Book. But really he was simply the head bookkeeper, not an accountant. Even so this is a position of respect and trust. He started out as a carpenter working with his dad and brothers. He became a bookkeeper and joined the Blank Book Company shortly after it opened in 1887. He was also a church and town leader, serving on many church boards and civic committees. Annetta, his wife, was also employed by the paper company, briefly, when she was still a teenager, but they met through the church. When they married, they were both about 19 years old.

My grandmother, Annetta Mauk Williams, was a Civil War orphan, born in May 1862. Her father, George W. Mauk, was a farmer. He was a 90 day enlistee - they were paid in cash and that tempted a farmer to put his plow aside. He enlisted in the Pennsylvania 125th Volunteers in July 1862. He got his crops in the ground, gave his signing bonus to his wife, Susan Frye Mauk, and went off to fight. His unit was trained just in time to muster, drill, and participate in the battle at Antietam on September 17, 1862. Twenty-three thousand Americans became casualties in that battle. George survived that terrible engagement in the cornfields at Antietam in September, but was injured and evacuated to the Soldiers Home in Washington DC, where he died of typhoid fever some months later.

This was the same Soldier's Home where President Lincoln kept a cottage as a retreat from the bustle and bother of the White House. He would ride out there and visit with the wounded. You can only wonder if George ever met the President during his months there. George's gravestone at the soldier's home in Washington DC says "MANK" on it. We've thought about getting a new marker, a new marker was offered because they were aware of the misspelling, caused by that copperplate script clerks used to keep records. A "u" mistaken for an "n." But the old markers are simple and worn with age, and that makes them special, even if his name is wrong.

**"GW Mank" grave marker. At the Soldier's Home, Washington, DC**

Susan Frye Mauk was then a Civil War widow with two small children and a "farewell baby," Annetta, who became my grandmother, called "Nettie." This was a time when potential Pennsylvania husbands were scarcer than hen's teeth!

When Susan remarried, she chose a man from a large family that was also well-settled in and around Roaring Spring: John B.

Myers. John Myers refused to raise another man's children, and Susan agreed to that when they married.

And so George Mauk's three children grew up in orphanages! There were hard feelings over this, even 60 years later when I was a boy. It was always stated with disgust: *he refused to raise another man's children.* It was said that Myers never sent much assistance to the orphans either and never treated them as family—even when they left the orphanage. The feeling was that John Myers could have done more, and the whole Myers family could have done more, but they treated the Mauk children poorly and let them go to the Civil War Orphanage.

The James Shane Williams Family, in front of their home at 45 East Main st, Roaring Spring, PA. In back: Clara, Ross, George, and Edwin. In front: Glenn, James Shane, Byron, Carl, Annetta, Paul, Merrill, and Mary Lillian, known as Lillian and called "MeMe" by her grandchildren.

About this photo, Mother said she had a new party dress, stockings, and shoes bought for her to wear for the photo and she simply refused to put her old coat on over her new dress! The family indulged her greatly and her older brother, nearly 20 years older, put his arms around her to keep her warm while they posed.

By the turn-of-the-century James Shane Williams was a prominent citizen in Roaring Spring. The Williams family had been part of the town for over 40 years. As I mentioned, Lillian's family was a large one. She was the tenth of 12 children: four girls and eight boys. Eight children survived both parents. Two girls died when they were still children and two boys died as young men. Meme was the last to go in 1994. She thought Jesus had forgotten about her.

Annetta died of kidney failure when I was still a small boy, but I have some memories of her. I remember working alongside her in her Roaring Spring vegetable garden. She'd give me a big spoon to and turn me loose in her vegetable garden where I'd dig the potatoes for her. She'd let me get nice and dirty. She had raised eight boys, so she understood them. You can't help but wonder if the 12 children born over 23 years might have been the real cause of her early death.

The James Shane Williams family lived just a few blocks up East Main Street from the Roaring Spring Blank Book Company, where James Shane worked. It was a small town when I knew it, maybe 3,000 people in total. It was centered around the

**Mary Lillian Williams Kinzer,**
**1900-1994**

paper mill, railroads, and the commercial establishments that lined Main St. Roaring Spring is important to my family. From 1866 on we had, within a small radius, the workplaces, the family church, and all the family homes for three generations of the Williams family - and the Mauk and Gilliland families too, all of them are in Roaring Spring.

Grandfather Williams had a comfortable life centered on his family, his church, and his work. He was never wealthy, but he was well-established and respected. Late in his life, as he was dying of prostate cancer, he lost much of his money in the stock market crash. He was especially invested in the aviation company Curtiss-Wright, still in business today. He had no business investing in the stock market but in the 1920s everyone in America had "stock fever."

JAMES S. WILLIAMS

TheWilliams boys I knew were George, Merrill, Ed, Byron, Glenn and Carl. Glenn was a pharmacist and Ed was a chemist with a graduate degree from Penn State. Ed was "too worldly" for his family, which meant he drank, gambled at cards, and liked a pool hall - all of these were great sins according to my starchy Methodist relatives.

Merrill was a Doctor of Divinity and George was the well-respected head of the mathematics department at Altoona High School, including when I was a student there. Merrill and George were the two pillars of the next generation, as I think about them, but they had no children, and in fact, made rather poor marriages. Merrill married Carrie Withington when they were both in their mid-30s and she was a few years older than him. Uncle George also married later, he was nearly 40 when he married Lucretia Myers.

Those four uncles Merrill, Ed, George, and Glenn were the high-achievers in that family, all were well-educated professionals.

Paul is the one I almost forgot. He was 20 and a machinist when he died in an automobile accident coming home from his job in

Altoona. He hit a tree and died the next day of internal injuries. The tree, a large oak near Hollidaysburg, was always pointed out whenever a family member drove past it. This was a tragedy that hit the whole family hard.

The other brother I never met was Ross. Ross is a bit of a mystery. The family didn't talk about him.

James Shane with seven of his eight sons, around 1915 Merrill, the oldest boy, is missing.

The Williams' were towns-people. My impression of them is that they thought they were rather better than they actually were. They had incomes and better educations and better starts. That's all that sets them apart from the Kinzers.

Dickinson College was nearby and my Williams ancestors favored Dickinson for their formal education. Most of my Williams had degrees from Dickinson - Paul and Byron were the two exceptions I know of. My Mother studied at Shippensburg, then called a Normal School, for a year of training to become a teacher.

I don't know how my parents met, but they did. Mother was employed as a school teacher in Roaring Spring, and living at home when they met. Mother enjoyed children and she loved interacting with them. She was firm but never strict, she was an "encourager" and always loving, so she would have made a good grade school teacher.

But she couldn't have been a teacher for long, because my parents married in December of 1922, on Christmas Day. Christmas day weddings were a Williams family tradition. There was a family reunion of sorts, a "home-coming" for that sacred day. With the family all in town and a big meal planned, it made a lot of sense to get married on that day, following services, in the family church.

After they married my parents, Brooks and Lillian, lived in Allentown, PA, where Brooks worked as a draftsman for the Bethlehem Steel Company. I was born in 1924, and Joanne was born in 1929. They were young adults, newlyweds, and loved the life they were making in Allentown. Mother and father always spoke fondly of those early years.

# Roaring Spring.

## KINZER—WILLIAMS

One of the prettiest church weddings ever witnessed in this town took place in the Methodist Episcopal church at 11 o'clock Christmas day, when the pastor, Rev. George A. Duvall, united in the holy bonds of matrimony Miss Lillian Williams, of Roaring Spring, and Brooks Kinzer, of Pittsburg. Just before the bridal party entered the church, Miss Elizabeth Garber, a close friend of the bride, sang "O Promise Me," after which while Miss Margaret Garber played Lohengrin's wedding march, the bride and groom and their attendants approached the altar, Miss Williams on her father's arm, and her brother, George B., of Altoona, with Mr. Kinzer as groom's man.

The bride wore a beautiful gown of pearl satin, lace veil and orange blossom head dress, and carried a shower bouquet of white roses; her maid of honor, Miss Kathryn Kinzer, of Llyswen, the groom's sister, carried an arm bouquet of pink roses. The bride's four brothers Glenn, Carol, Edward and Byron were ushers. Miss Williams is the accomplished daughter of Mr. and Mrs. James S. Williams, of East Main street, and one of the successful grade teachers in the local public school. She will finish her school work for the year before going to housekeeping. Mr. Kinzer is a son of Mr. and Mrs. William Kinzer, of Reed's Gap, Juniata county, and is employed in the engineering department of the Pressed Steel Car company, of McKees Rocks. Both are popular members of the younger set and a host of friends wish them much happiness throughout their married life.

After the ceremony Mr. and Mrs. Williams entertained the bride and groom and intimate friends and relatives at a sumptuous turkey dinner at their beautiful East Main street home.

Wedding Announcement, December 1922

Brooks and Lillian returned to Roaring Spring often so they could visit Mother's family. Annetta was failing and Mother would get called home to take care of Nettie, they were close. In general Nettie was as loved by her children as James Shane was feared. Lilllian went back and forth to Roaring Spring taking me (a baby) along with her and traveling by train.

**Annetta Mauk Williams, 1862-1930, probably in the 1910s**

At some point my grandfather, James Shane Williams, who was very much the patriarch, even when he was old and sick, *decided* that Lillian would be her parents' caretaker. Brooks agreed to this arrangement, leaving his work as a draftsman with Bethlehem Steel and moving the family to Roaring Spring. This was in 1927 or 1928. I think I must have been about four when we moved back to Roaring Spring.

As I think about it, my parents gave up a lot to return home. They were very happy in Allentown, and Roaring Spring was more complicated for them.

Annetta Mauk Williams died of kidney failure in 1930, when I was about 6, leaving James Shane Williams slowly dying of prostate cancer. He died in 1932. *[Both of Dad's grandfathers died that year.]*

**Annetta Mauk Williams, "Nettie," in the 1920s**

George "Shorty" Williams, my uncle, was head of the mathematics department at Altoona High School, where I was a student. I never shamed him, and always did my best as a student and an athlete. George became the "head of the family" after grandfather passed. Merrill, who was older, was working his way through the ranks of the Methodist Ministry and wasn't close by. They move Ministers around every few years. By 1930 George was well-settled in his career at Altoona High School and had stayed closely-tied to his father.

Another uncle was Edwin, or Ed. He was a good friend of Izat and Grace Humer (more about them later). He was also a Penn State graduate, in chemistry, but had a low-paying, unambitious kind of job in Pittsburgh. When he decided to go on a toot, he would spend the weekend with the Humers. Ed was an embarrassment to the family due to his drinking, and he was told by Grandfather to keep his drinking out of Roaring Spring - and he did! Sally Humer *[the daughter of Izat and Grace—a school friend of Dad's]* and I once saw Ed falling-down drunk at a parade in Altoona, a sight I will never forget! *[There's a little of that Williams' family primness coming through in Jim Kinzer!]*

When I told my folks what I had seen, my mother said, "... it started early, when he was at Penn State, and, my-oh-my, how Mother pleaded with him to get his life straight." Ed's wife was Alfaretta. She was a World War I widow with a son named Jimmy Kagy.

There were other brothers in addition to George and Ed. Merrill, the oldest, was a Methodist minister. He was married to Carrie, a stern woman, older than him. Merrill had choice assignments, so he must have been a good minister, but it wasn't a good marriage. My guess is that Merrill was told to marry or his career would stall…and I'm also guessing they both died virgins. But as I said, Merrill had a good career and in the late 1940s he was rewarded with a final assignment back in Roaring Spring at the family church. He officiated at my wedding to Snippy Doodle.

Glen was a pharmacist in Philadelphia, a committed fan of the Eagles and the Phillies. When he came home from Philadelphia to visit, he'd come by train, it was always a good time for the whole family. Dr. Lambert was the Roaring Spring pharmacist who encouraged Glen to get a degree in pharmacy. Glen was eventually induced to take over Lambert's drugstore. That's when he moved back to Roaring Spring with his wife, Evelyn. She was from Martinsburg and her father was a physician named "Bonebreaker" of all the nearly-impossible names for a physician. Their children were Glen Jr. and Sally. This was one of the happy marriages in the Williams clan - they were all social and fun. Glen was never the same after he returned to Roaring Spring; Philadelphia had been his "happy hunting ground" where he had independence and privacy and lived a more sophisticated life than was available in Roaring Spring.

My uncle Byron Williams was a disabled veteran of World War I. Shrapnel had destroyed one lung and damaged the other. The battle was at Chateau Thierry. He raised and trained registered beagle dogs, which he sold throughout Pennsylvania, West Virginia, Virginia, and New York. Within the hunting-dog world, Byron was famous. His dogs were prized for both breeding and their careful training.

Carl was the youngest in the family, he was born to Annetta when she was in her 40s. He left college to marry Hazel Kemberlin, a love match. They had four children and struggled through the Depression.

Like all big families living in close proximity, there was a tendency to be too much in the affairs of others, their drinking, money problems, employment, and marriages. Mother was closest to her younger brothers - Glenn and Carl - and all three families lived in Roaring Spring when I was a boy there.

My grandfather Williams was generous with his family. They had a generous Christmas - with a big meal, and gifts of clothing and books and toys, and gold coins were handed out too. But then he was almost ruined by the stock market crash and the Depression. I think, but do not know for certain, that it was my Father's money, he was repaying a loan made by James Shane in better times, that kept the old man afloat in his last years of life

Grandfather knew nothing about investing, but he got the bug like everyone else, and had purchased Curtis-Wright common stock. The stock tanked but the shares still had some value and the family worked hard to keep the shares, hoping for a comeback.

Lillian "Meme" Kinzer with her brothers: Merrill, Glenn, Carl, Ed, George, and Byron Williams. Mother was very small, as was Annetta, who she resembled in many other ways. Both were gentle, indulgent, and good-humored. (Family photo from the mid 1940's)

Carl and Mother, being the younger children and both living in Roaring Spring, were close. Carl and Hazel, his wife, and my cousins, were over to our house often, especially for Sunday supper, just after church. I remember Uncle Carl coming to our house in Roaring Spring, requesting Dad to drive him to Altoona to prevail upon his older brother George, the executor of their father's estate. Carl wanted George to sell enough Curtis-Wright stock to see his family through another month. There was a heated argument over this. Carl was desperate and George was sympathetic, but didn't want to fight with his wife Lucretia, who was very much against selling any of the stock.

So George dragged his feet, not refusing but never exactly selling the stock either. Carl was distraught. Hazel, Carl's wife, peeled their potatoes so thin the peelings were transparent! "Let the others help him!" Lucretia said. She had George boxed in tight.

At Christmastime Lucretia gave *one* mallow cup to my sister JoAnn and one to me. Mallow cups were an Altoona product. She bought them wholesale at the factory, and they came in a two-pack. She was definitely not a spendthrift! The family all loved and respected George, but no one liked dealing with Lucretia.

I am recalling now that my Uncle George would often pursue continuing education, to "advance myself" he would say. He found educational opportunities every summer, sometimes at State College, sometimes at Dickenson, leaving Lucretia for a month or two, and I take that as another sign the marriage was not a happy one.

What Brooks thought of all this family drama, I don't know. He was a quiet man, circumspect, but with a sharp eye, so I don't think he missed much of what was going on around him, even if he was inclined to keep his thoughts to himself.

He lived among his wife's people and had accepted that condition. Brooks doted on Mother, she was his prize - educated, refined, and good-humored. They were a nice match, since Brooks tended to be serious and quiet. If he came home in a bad mood, a few minutes with Mother always lightened him. And if Mother was a little spoiled, that suited Father, too. He liked to indulge her, he always bought her whatever she wanted, she had a fur coat and pearls, new dresses every year. He wanted her to have an easy life, easier than he had known and easier than the life his mother had. He wanted to provide that.

# THE KINZERS AND KIRKS OF REEDS GAP

Reeds Gap is on Pennsylvania Hwy. 35 between Shade Gap and Mifflintown where the highway crosses the Juniata River. The Gap was part of the warpath the Iroquois Indians (Mohawk) followed on their raids into Virginia and Maryland. This is a very rural area, even today, with houses and small farms spread out along two-lane roads that follow the creeks and passes

By the time Dad joined them, his family had lived in the area for well over 100 years, and he was directly related to many of the people that were neighbors to his grandparents: Kinzer, Kirk, Lauver, Harris, Murphy, Buchanan, Crawford, and Bollinger. Germans, English, and Scots...spirited frontiersmen making new homes in the Pennsylvania Wilderness. In the 1930s when Dad spent his summers here, the area still had one foot planted firmly in the 19th century.

I liked the Kinzers more than I liked the Williamses. The Kinzers were very aware of their background and talked about their ancestors and relations all the time. Their lives were more interesting to me too - or the way they lived was more interesting. Every day on a farm is a lesson you can carry with you for the rest of your life. They welcomed me, their grandson and nephew, into their lives and the lives of the generations before them.

The Kinzers are Palatinate Protestant settlers from Germany - not Hessian Soldiers as so many of the Pennsylvania Dutch were. They came to Pennsylvania after William Penn and his agents visited the Rhine provinces to encourage immigration and assured them they would enjoy religious freedom once they fought off the Indians.

The Kinzer/Kinser/Kintzers arrived about 1729 or so, sailing from Holland. They landed in Philadelphia and settled in Earl Township, part of Lancaster County. There is a town called Kinzers, not too far from Philadelphia. There was a doctor and a state senator in the early family line, so they seem to have been well-qualified people.

But the Kinzers of Reeds Gap were modest people with modest achievements. For generations they were subsistence farmers, dating back to the start of our country. (The 1790 US Census shows a cluster of Kinzers: David, John, George and Valentine in Earl, Lancaster County, only a few miles from Juniata and Mifflin counties.)

The Juniata is a historic river. Its headwaters are in Bedford, Pennsylvania running westward to Pittsburgh and on to the Ohio River. The Gap, literally a gap in the mountains, joined Reeds Gap with Black Log and Black Log Creek, extending northwest to the trail leading to Fort Shirley.

An ancestor of mine, David Gilliland, served in the American rebellion. He was stationed at Fort Roberdeau, just north of Altoona, guarding against Iroquois incursions that were allied with the British during the Rebellion of the American Colonies. The Iroguois were masters at shifting allegiances.

My great-grandfather, William, married Mary Ann Murphy in 1847. I was always told that she was several steps up in the social class ladder. *[Mary Ann Murphy Kinzer, 1826-1904, I find William and Mary as young marrieds in the 1850 Census, living in Lack, just outside Reeds Gap.]*

I do not know how or why my great-grandfather, William Alexander Kinzer, came to be in Juniata County. He married Mary Anne Murphy, the Murphys were numerous; her family was well-settled in Reeds Gap. They would not have married their daughter to a man they didn't know and like, so however William Alexander Kinzer came to be in Reeds Gap, we can assume that he was liked and trusted. You don't just hand over a daughter to a stranger.

He was probably a descendant of the Kinzers already established in Lancaster. I say "probably" because my sister Jo Ann worked on this lineage and never could prove the direct connection. He would likely have traveled by water up the Susquehanna to Harrisburg, taking the Juniata River west to Port Royal, where the Tuscarora Creek joins the Juniata River from the Juniata Valley. *[I have also failed to establish William Kinzer's origins before he arrived in Reeds Gap and married Mary Anne Murphy. He was probably a descendant of the Kinzers in Port Royal.]*

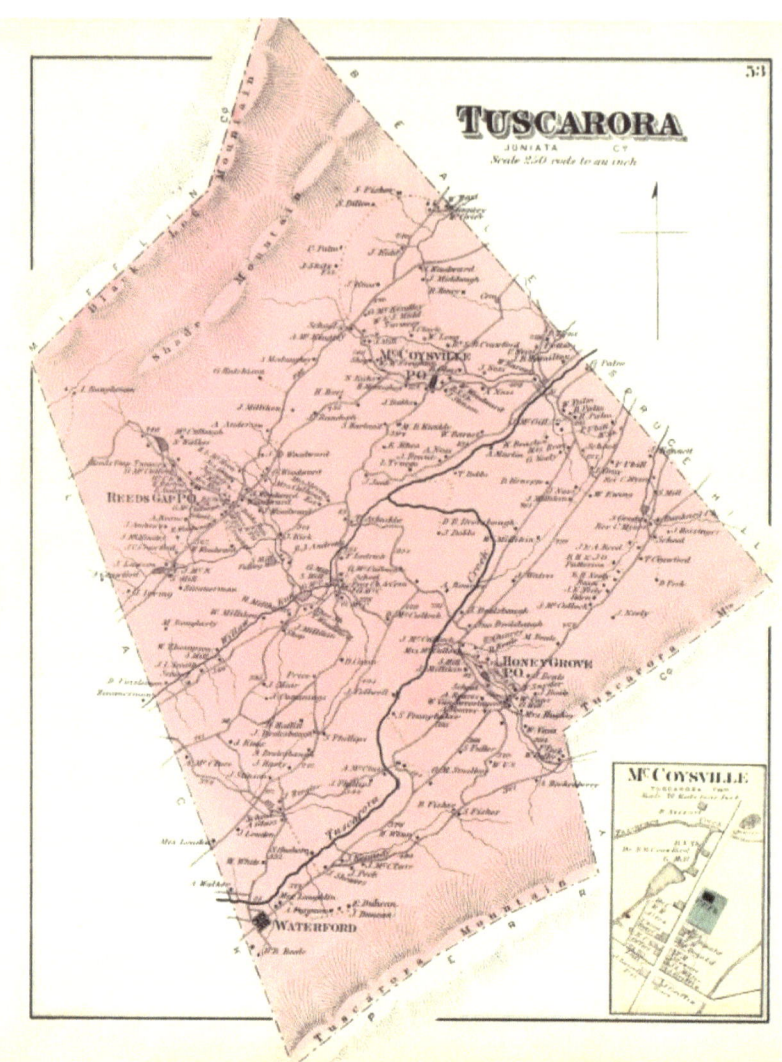

Reeds Gap in 1877. The property near the center labeled *J. Kirk* is probably the farm given to Maggie Kirk when she married Will Kinzer. [Library of Congress Digital Map Collection]

William Kinzer served in the Union Army, 173rd Regiment, Pennsylvania Volunteers, in 1862 and 1863, He was 39 when he joined and had six or seven, maybe eight, children at home. In the weeks following Gettysburg, the 173rd chased Lee south and guarded the rail lines in the summer of 1863. He died in August 1864, almost a year after his service, but it isn't clear if he was injured in battle or just died young, as farmers did.

His widow, Mary Ann Murphy Kinzer, drew a pension when the war was over. If he had been injured in battle, surely it would have been spoken of, so my guess is that he simply died young the way poor people do. We don't know much about him. His headstone is at the cemetery at McCullochs Mills, but it doesn't say anything more. So he's a mystery.

I knew all the Murphys when I was a kid. They had a nice farm in Reeds Gap, and other Murphys were up Route 36. Families named Lauther/Lauver are in the area too, in Black Log. We were all related to each other by marriage and blood and the simple connection of proximity.

I knew my grandfather, William Alexander Kinzer, born in 1864. He was called Will, born just months before his father died. They were very poor people, living in a house little better than a log cabin in Reeds Gap/Lack. Their small farm was right up next to another, much better farm, owned by the Murphys.

My grandfather, Will, was good-looking, a lean and healthy young man with a handle-bar mustache and a head of black, wavy, hair. His sister, my Aunt Elizabeth Kinzer, was good-looking too, with a strong family resemblance.

Will was a quiet man, serious and purposeful. Up early, facing a long hard day going from one task to the next, all of it physical work, and then early to bed. As I learned, Farm Folk follow the sun. The sun goes down, you finish up your chores, have a wash, eat dinner, say "good night" and take a candle to your bed. Not like at home where Mother would clear away supper and then make some coffee and they would listen to the radio while Father read the paper and Mother did mending.

Will married Margaret Lauther Kirk, known as Maggie. He married well, too. He "married up," as we say. I know this for a fact, because one day while driving in the area, my father, Brooks, pointed out where his father was born. My Grandparent's farmhouse was a modest affair, but this was no more than a one-room log cabin, not too far from Reeds Gap—maybe five miles west on Route 36 from Shade's Gap to Mifflintown.

I think Brooks wanted me to understand where Will came from and why he was the way he was. He told me Will grew up barefoot and the only Christmas Will knew was a half day of chores, time for church, and a better supper than usual.

Maggie was a Kirk and the Kirks were much better off. They had property in Reeds Gap, and just like the Murphys the Kirks had extended family throughout the area. An 1877 map of Tuscarora Township in Juniata County, PA shows a store and three additional "in-town" properties at the crossroads, all owned by the Kirk family. More than one farm in the immediate area was owned by a Kirk.

**Margaret Kirk Kinzer (1872-1950), seated in the front with some of her Port Royal relatives. Behind Margaret, wearing eye glasses, is Elizabeth Kinzer Bollinger (1860-1940), Maggie's sister-in-law. Will Crawford is one over from Ella Crawford. The family resemblance is evident. The photo may have been taken in 1898, about the time Maggie married Will Kinzer.**

The Kirks, Murphys, Bollingers, and Crawfords were all related to each other. This is the way of rural living: you can only court and marry someone you have met after all. You might "meet" a girl through church, school, or at a social, but most likely you had already known her all your life because she was a neighbor.

Will and Maggie were married in 1898. The Kirks were not exactly happy about Maggie marrying a poor man from a poor family, but she was 26, unmarried, and very much in love with Will Kinzer, who was ten years older.

Margaret Kirk Kinzer was a strong-willed and determined woman. She ran the family and their finances while Will ran the farm. But she never scolded or nagged. Will was poor and profane, but a hard worker and a good man with those country manners, that I grew fond of. Unassuming people, polite, humble. Respectful.

One Christmas, I was a little disappointed with my "haul" and Father chided me, saying that there were many Christmases when he was growing up when they got nothing more than what was needed: socks, some pencils, a new winter coat. As a boy my Grandfather Will didn't even get that much, that's why he was so glad for a special dinner following Christmas services.

**Maggie and Will Kinzer about 1903, with Brooks and Catherine.**

Their first child was my dad, born 13 months after they married. James Brooks Kinzer, called Brooks. The James part is from James Kirk, Maggie's father and the family benefactor. Dad was not a high school graduate and because he had pleurisy he could not serve in WWI. *[According to his WWI Draft card Brooks completed sixth grade, only.]*

Barely out of his teens, Maggie sent Brooks away from the farm where he'd been living and working, to a technical school in DC, where he lived in a boarding house for the year of training. I don't know where the money came from, probably from the Kirks. Brooks was a smart man, though uneducated, and quickly employed as a draftsman for the Pennsylvania Railroad.

Maggie recognized Brooks would have a better life if he was not a farmer. She wanted more for each of her children, and was good at setting goals and making a plan for that. She encouraged my dad to get out of Reeds Gap and do better for himself. I visited a classmate of my father's in DC when I was in law school there myself. The fellow's name was Bill Snowe, he was full of praise for Brooks. He saw the same qualities in Brooks that Maggie recognized.

My Aunt Catherine was born in 1901, two years after my dad was born. The story is that Maggie put Brooks through draftsman school. Then he repaid his mother by using some of his draftsman wages to put his sister Catherine through teacher's college. The plan was that Catherine would then put her younger brother, Byron, through teacher's college. Instead, she married Lehman Kirk, a neighbor and distant relation. She was briefly employed as a teacher and so was Lehman when they courted and married. Lehman refused to hand over any of Catherine's wages, so Byron never went to college.

Lehman served overseas in WWI and played first base for the Waterford baseball team. He was a country boy who did all right owning a store in East Waterford. He was also a champion checker player. The Lehman Kirks lived nearby the Will Kinzers, and our families socialized, so I knew all my Kirk cousins.

My dad's immediate family were Brooks, Catherine Kinzer Lehman (1901-1994) and his younger brothers, Byron (Byron Rosell Kinzer, 1909-1969) and Bivon (William C. Bivon Kinzer, 1914-1969).

I have no explanation for the gap between the two oldest children and the two younger ones.

**Dad, about one year old, held by William Alexander Kinzer, his grandfather, at the Kinzer family farm in Reeds Gap—probably early summer 1925. You can see the two-story farmhouse with a summer kitchen (shed) and the bank barn in the background.**

Will Kinzer was a profane man and God-fearing. He'd swear up a storm in the barn yard and then pray long and loud on his knees in church.

Their farm had a small orchard, and Will was also a beekeeper. I remember his colony swarming to the cherry tree instead of his hive, and Grandfather carefully picking through the mass of bees trying to find the Queen Bee to draw them all back. As he did it, he explained it to me. Will didn't talk a lot and his conversations were usually about the weather, his farm, or his faith.

He liked to hear about my day, though. After I was done with my chores I'd go out adventuring and he liked to hear about what I got up to. I don't think he was particularly literate, but he had enough schooling to read his bible. Maggie had more schooling and she read the daily newspaper as well as her bible.

I also remember my Grandfather Kinzer driving a truck and hauling wood during the Depression. For the money. He was an old man, well past 70 and still chopping, delivering, and stacking a truckload of firewood! Those were hard years, but of course a farmer's life is just one hard year after another. When I was in Reeds Gap you never heard much about the rest of the world. No one talked about the headlines or politics or the economy. You talked about the weather and you talked about your farm.

Maggie Kinzer taught Sunday school and prepared Communion services. She took service to her church seriously. Byron Kinzer, her son, passed the collection plate. On the occasion of Communion, Maggie served dinner to the itinerant preacher who administered Communion. On those occasions Will didn't "sasser" his coffee—tipping it from the cup to the saucer to sip from - nor did he eat his peas with his knife. The dinner she served was always marvelous, "Preacher's Meat," pork loin was always the main course, and there would be pie and ice cream with coffee.

Maggie had a brother, Charles Kirk, who lived a poor sort of life at a rented place. He owned a truck and painting gear with ladders hanging off the sides, and painted barns in better times. His wife was Frances; they had a good-looking family. I remember going to their place on a ridge near Reeds Gap where we picked dewberries and cherries for pie-making.

He had it hard during the Depression. Great Uncle Charles painted barns for a living and Bivon sometimes worked with him. Now, a farmer needs his barn and the barn needs paint so it is steady work, even in bad times, but it doesn't pay well. They made 50 cents each a day for painting. For fifty cents a day in cash, they counted themselves lucky.

Great-uncle Charlie and my Aunt Frances had a very pretty daughter, Dolly *[Dorothy, born about 1911.]* She lived in Pittsburgh; perhaps that's why they all moved there. She was married to a WWI survivor who had a metal plate in his head. I was fascinated by it, seeing his skin stretched over the metal plate, pulsing with his heartbeat. Charles couldn't earn a living, and couldn't support his family.

Eventually he packed the truck with everything they owned and moved to Pittsburgh, joining his daughter Dolly and her husband, to start over. It's a story right out of *The Grapes of Wrath!*

Dolly was a beauty, and I have always been drawn to a pretty girl. I remember she and my grandmother criticizing the Montgomery Ward and Sears Roebuck and Company catalogs for picturing women in lingerie; it was disgusting to them. But those catalogs served another, better purpose to keep on hand, so to speak, in the outhouse.

I knew my other great-uncles, Maggie's brothers: Bayles Kirk, who owned rental property in Altoona, and Samuel C. Kirk, who lived in Columbus, Ohio. Sam married well and I spent a summer with them.

These were poor times *[1930-1939.]* Groceries? They were often bartered, milk was a nickel a quart, a loaf of bread was a dime, and six gallons of gas cost a dollar. Cigarettes were ten cents a pack and everyone collected coupons, inside the pack, to get a free pack.

My Kinzer uncles could repair anything that moved - wagons, autos, trucks - and they spent many weekends fixing neighbors' cars and trucks, in return for gas money or in exchange for food.

Brooks, besides being a draftsman, was a good butcher. He was good at many different jobs, as were his father and brothers. Farm life forces you to apply yourself to any situation. As I think back on those years, Brooks was always employed and made good money. He was in great demand during deer hunting season and when the hogs are slaughtered for the winter. He would trade his butchering for a share of the meat.

I remember seeing Brooks at work weighing meat in the grocery store he owned in Roaring Spring. I would have been a small boy then. He stopped working as a butcher, but kept that business through the Depression, collecting rent, and then later he sold it. Brooks also managed a bigger grocery store in Altoona, Schaffers Store; they were a Jewish family and owned a few stores in the area. The Schaffers trusted Brooks to run their biggest store and, later, he also managed their store in Martinsburg. They trusted him with two of their stores!

While running his own store in Roaring Spring, he began selling burial insurance, on the side. The premiums were 50 cents or a dollar. It was the simplest form of insurance—just a ledger and a receipt book. But people placed a lot of trust in the man who would see to your funeral expenses. His collection route took him deep into the hollows of Mifflin and Juniata County, where the name "Kinzer" was well known and trusted. Through selling burial insurance, he eventually became an insurance salesman for Prudential, staying with them until just before he died at 65. *[Our brother.John remembers going on "Insurance Runs" with Poppy, driving deep into the countryside.. John would play with their dogs and pick cherries while Brooks spoke with his clients on their porch. Chatting was an important part of the visit. And then the handing over of money. Poppy making notes in his ledger and then handing them a receipt.*

I remember my dad fondly. He was always supportive, encouraging, and kind to me. You could talk things through with him and he would listen and give his observations - he was a good study of human nature and his opinions were valuable. He wanted me to have what he hadn't had, but he didn't spoil me or baby me. When he dropped me off at the farm it was not a summer vacation, far from it: he expected me to contribute and be useful to his parents.

Brooks was a combination of his parents. Physically, he resembled his Dad, but otherwise, he was very much like his mother - intelligent and determined. He was a first-class gentleman, a great Christian, naturally intelligent, always honest, and of high moral standards. He had those good country manners I still admire, unassuming and quiet, soft-spoken but firm, firm in his word and his convictions. He understood human nature, both good and bad. Other people saw those qualities too.

Father had the most beautiful blue eyes, and what a pity that no one in the family got those blue eyes!

Brooks would have conversations with me when I was a boy. He spoke to me in an intelligent way. He was always open and frank, never talking down to me. Children are smarter than we think, and Brooks knew that, and I tried to do that as a father, too. I would see so many fathers talking down to their kids or being mean to them – putting them down, yelling at them, shaking them. I never wanted to fall into that, and I hope I was a gentle father - a quality I saw in Brooks and Will.

I had more respect for Father than I did for the Williamses. I often thought the Williamses thought they were too good for Roaring Spring.

Brooks' father was little more than a dirt poor farmer, but Will was a hard worker. There were times when Will ran a very small store as well as farming. He sold only staple foods: candy and canned goods. He also operated a post office and collected taxes for a while. They patched their living together from the farm and many odd jobs. Brooks was a lot like Will, a quiet man and a hard worker, they were men who accepted their lot in life and bore it well.

A few years after she was widowed, in about 1937, Margaret Kirk and Uncle Bivon sold the farm and moved to Mercersburg, PA, where there was a state teacher's college. Bivon, 23 or so, was the last child at home. Maggie, in her 60s, worked as a clerk at the college, waited tables and took in laundry in order to see to Bivon's education. As I said, she was a determined woman and wanted every opportunity possible for her children. She wanted Brooks to be a draftsman, Clara to be a teacher, and she thought Bivon should be a teacher, too. *[In the 1940 Census, Margaret, 67, lived with her youngest son, W.C. Bivon Kinzer, age 25. Bivon taught school, having graduated from teachers college. He married the next year, in 1941.]*

Maggie spent her last years living with her daughter, Catherine, and her family in East Waterford. She died after a fall in the summer of 1950. Snippy was pregnant, and due any day, so I could not attend. Maggie was important to me and I missed her funeral. I still feel bad about that. But we drove up later in the summer, to visit and show off our new baby.

Uncle Byron Kinzer was my favorite. He told me many stories about the Indians who had lived here and Indian lore. He showed me their traditional paths in the hills and coves, and always had time for my questions. He taught me how to use and keep guns and took me out on the road with him while he worked, letting me be his helper. Brooks and Byron were cut from the same cloth.

Byron was fortunate to have paying work, but he had a tough job. He was a lineman for the telephone company. He put up telephone poles all by himself, all through Juniata County. He dug the hole, put up the poles, secured it, put on the cross arms, and hung the wires. He was paid 25 cents an hour and was trusted to keep his own time cards. It was hard work; he used dynamite regularly, and one time he got a terrible gash on his right forearm from a broken insulator.

I went along with him two or three times. I was always excited at night when I knew I would be out on the road with him the next morning. Grandmother would pack lunch buckets for each of us.

When there was a new subscriber, Uncle Byron would run the line to the house and install the phone. He would get an order for a new hook-up and run the line from the main road to the house. The telephones were large and mounted on the wall. These were still the crank phones, indicating the calling number in short and long cranks. They were all party lines. There was no privacy, but I'm guessing neither was there trespass. You could listen to anyone's call…if it was worth listening to, I can't say.

The Kinzers didn't have a phone, or a radio, electricity, or running water in that house. Living in the country like my grandparents meant cooking was done on a wood-burning stove. (Mother had a proper range and refrigerator at home.)

In the summer, I was expected to keep the tinderbox next to the stove stocked with small pieces of wood that would fit into a wood stove. Byron and Bivon stocked the woodshed, but I helped by splitting the wood meant just for the stove from wood kept in the wood shed. I loved using the ax and the hatchet.

The stove had a little metal vessel set into a holder on the side. If you wanted hot water to wash up with you took the vessel to the pump, filled it with water and set it back in the holder. That was my job too. It held about two gallons - a lot for an eight-year old boy to carry, but there are good lessons to be had in carrying water. We had to wait awhile for the hot stove to heat up the water, but that's how we got hot water for washing-up.

The house in Reeds Gap was a classic "I-house," that was small, just four rooms, but better than a log cabin.. The kitchen was downstairs, along with a living room heated by a Franklin stove. There was no dining room; we ate in the kitchen. There were two bedrooms upstairs: one for Will and Maggie, and the other was a kind of bunkhouse for Byron, Bivon, and whoever else was staying there. Me. The house never had electricity. *[We saw it in the summer of 2009 and the second floor was gone. It appeared to be a hunting lodge then. An expanded wood shed and outhouse were still there.]*

We used kerosene lamps at Grandmother Kinzer's. That was another one of my chores. I was given the small job of trimming the wicks in the oil lamps, cleaning the globes when they got sooty and refilling the kerosene. Once I burned my hand badly grabbing a globe that wasn't yet cooled. My grandfather used some kind of country salve and bandaged me up.

There was one chandelier-sized lamp hanging over the kitchen table. It had a so-called mantle, thin, fragile, and gauze-like. There was a large oil lamp in the parlor, which also shed light from a mantle. The mantle allowed for a smaller flame and less soot, so we didn't have to clean those big ceiling lamps so often. The lamp oil was stored in the base. There was a plunger for a very large lamp we pumped to force the vapor up into the mantle, whereupon the mantle would start to provide light. A valve slowly opened to feed more fuel into the mantle, and once sufficiently warmed, the mantle cast a strong pleasant light. Mantles were expensive, and great care was taken not to puncture one with a match, or let it burst into flames. That was all the light there was in that house once darkness set in.

The simple application of this technology and the way it worked fascinated me. In Roaring Spring we had light switches. In Reeds Gap we had oil lamps and flames, and I preferred that because you could look at the mechanism and figure out what each component did.

There were pictures and mementos on display in the parlor, the nicest room in the house. Uncle Byron had awards from a Civilian Conservation Corps training camp. The awards were for track and marksmanship. In the kitchen, Byron had a chest where he kept his guns and cleaning equipment. The smell from the chest was simply splendid to me. *[Indeed, we all know how much dad loved the smell of gun oil.]* I smell those things now and I think of Uncle Byron and happy times.

Uncle Bivon was only 10 years older than I was, and there was a bit of a rivalry between us. I remember one time when I was six or seven, climbing up the steep stairs at night and Bivon popped out of a closet wearing a white sheet. I was so scared I fell back down the stairs and I still remember Margaret Kirk giving Bivon a whipping for it. "Bivon, you dasn't do things like that to Jimmy!" "Dasn't" was the word she used.

Those stairs were narrow and steep. Maggie called the stairs the "wooden hill." She'd say, "I'm going to climb the wooden hill," which meant she was going to bed.

There was no plumbing in that house. We used a wash basin and a chamber pot, or the outhouse - you learned to "regulate yourself!" I remember when Uncle Byron replaced the outhouse. He had to blast a new hole with dynamite and then he built the new outhouse. I thought Uncle Byron could do anything.

Once school was out I spent the entire summer in Reeds Gap with the Kinzers every year from 1930 to 1937, age six to 13. I stayed with them all summer long. Father would drive me out not long after school let out, and he'd pick me up again just in time to buy new shoes and clothes for school.

The farm at Reeds Gap was given to Maggie Kirk by her family when she married. It was located beside a dusty road leading through the mountain gap to Black Log, an historic site where pioneers and the Iroquois Indians tried to settle their affairs.

When I was at the farm in Reeds Gap, Brooks would drive out for visits off and on through the summer. He always brought loads of groceries for his mother and brothers. He bought things they didn't have the cash for - and they had very little cash. It wasn't like we had so much, but we had more and Brooks did what he could to make Maggie's life better.

Brooks would also take on projects at the farm. Between them, Brooks and Byron could do just about anything. Brooks made a raised wooden-plank walkway from the house to the outhouse to help his mother. He was driving stakes with the butt-end of a long-handled axe, and on the back swing he grazed my head. I had come up too close behind him, being curious, and the axe split my skin open about four inches! Brooks thought he'd split my skull completely, but it was just a scalp wound. Grandmother Kinzer was frantic, because there was so much blood.

A photo from the late 1940s showing Margaret Kirk Kinzer (1872-1950) at the family farm in Reeds Gap, with three of her children: Brooks, Catherine Kinzer Kirk, and Byron. Bivon, the youngest, may have taken this picture.

With a towel pressed to the top of my head, Dad drove me about five miles up the road to Dr. Ritter in McCoysville. He cleaned the wound and closed it up with tape. As I recall, there were no stitches. Everyone seemed to use that salve. They called it "drawing salve," but it was black and smelled like tar - Ichthammol, was what it was. That smell, I'd know it in a minute! There isn't much else to do with a wound like that. I still have the scar from that day, and I can feel it to this day, too, 80 years later. *[You could feel the little ridge along his scalp!]*

Those summers were wonderful. There were no safety measures; I had the axes, a BB gun, and a 22! I used a hatchet every day, and I was free to come and go once my chores were done. I had adventures all over the Gap. Kids might lose eyes or fingers, but now they lose their lives to drugs. Maybe the escapes we had were better than the escape they get from drugs.

Most transactions at the farm - and everywhere in Reeds Gap - were done through barter. We traded what *we had* for whatever *they had*. Grandmother had a hen house, and I had to chase the chickens off the nests to get fresh eggs right after they were laid. The hens didn't like it and they pecked and flapped at me. Also the hen house was close, hot and smelly, so I hated the job. But almost every day I took a dozen eggs to Murphy's farm about a mile away and swapped for fresh butter, because Maggie didn't have time for churning and the Murphy's had daughters to do it. Aside from pigs and chickens, the Kinzers kept one or two milk cows. Will or Bivon would milk the cows and set it aside for a dealer who came every day to collect it.

In the summer I had the job of slopping the pigs, and feeding them a sort of mealy gruel of collected food scraps. They were slaughtered in the fall, two or three yearly. Another job was moving the animals around, especially finding shade for them on hot days. Grandfather would tell me what to do - put those hogs back in the shed, take the horses out to the field, move the view to some shade. I did what I was told.

The hogs were slaughtered after school had started. My Dad would drive us out to the farm for a long weekend of hard work. It took two full busy days, with Brooks doing the butchering.

The slaughter was started by Uncle Byron, by letting the hogs out to the pen yard. Byron stunned each with a .22 shot to the head. Then he vaulted the fence and slit each hog's throat with his big Bowie knife, then vaulted quickly back out again! It took a while for the hogs to bleed to death and they were dangerous. I watched from the safe side of the fence, along with Dad, Bivon, and Grandfather. The hogs were left to bleed to death and then strung up to allow the last of the blood to drip out into a tub.

Meanwhile, we would set up big work tables where the hogs would be butchered, and the cauldron would be fired. We'd get the smokehouse ready too. I did whatever I was told, happy to be included working with the men.

The next day the hogs were scalded in a big cauldron over a fire. Then they were skinned and butchered into chops, loins, bacon, and other parts I can't remember. Maybe I was back home by then.

Sausage was made from mincing the liver, kidneys, lungs, heart, stomach etc. Grandmother would chop and grind and stuff the sausage into tubes of soaked and washed pig intestines. We used every bit of that hog.

The hams, sausage, and bacon were hung in the smokehouse and cured to serve our winter needs. The smell of the smokehouse interior was pungent and overwhelming. It brought tears to your eyes, it was so strong! There are no words to describe it.

After hog butchering was cleared away, Grandmother would use the ashes and rendered hog fat to make soap. It was hard work—another task that took a whole day or more. But it was the nicest soap you can imagine.

My mother bartered for some of that soap, always sending something from town that Grandmother needed, a new dress, handbag, or shoes in exchange for some of her soap. Meme was kind, too, always sending Maggie something extra nice for the exchange.

As a young boy, soap-making caused me some worry, because it took hours of boiling and I had to stay close by and feed the fire for her. She would stand at the fire, stirring her big cauldron, wearing her oldest dress, red faced and with her hair pinned-upcoming free from the hard work. Though of course I knew she was my grandmother, Maggie Kinzer looked just like a witch! The problem was I knew that witches cooked and ate little boys!

There was a grist mill at McCullochs Mills where Vaida is buried at Honey Grove. My marker is there, aswell as my grandparents'. The mill had a waterwheel, turned by the tumbling mill race. The race was a strong flow of water confined by stones that came from nearby Tuscarora Creek. The miller was Miller Thompson. I visited them one time with Uncle Byron. We had gathered in a room dimly lit by kerosene lamps. This was how people visited, with coffee boiled in a big kettle, a glass of cold milk for me, and maybe a plate of cookies or biscuits and butter.

Not far away was an ice house, where the ice was cut from the Tuscarora Creek in the wintertime and conserved within layers of sawdust. People paid to have ice cut and delivered to their kitchen.

Grandmother didn't have a refrigerator. She had an icebox only. Our mailbox was out in front of the farm by the street. It was just a dirt road, really. Your mailbox was there, of course, and attached to the post was a dial to turn to tell the iceman how much ice you wanted by the pound: 25, 50, 75 or 100 pounds of ice. It was my job to check the ice in the morning and set the dial. The ice truck was something I looked forward to. He'd cut the ice and carry it up to Maggie's kitchen and put it in her ice box. Usually he'd hack off a piece of ice for me.

The arrival of the iceman was a nice interruption each week. Maggie would invite him to visit, she'd make coffee, and he'd have news to report, having been in the home of every neighbor.

We used that ice to make ice cream, too. One summer we ate ice cream nearly every day. There was a heat wave and the milk would spoil before the dealer could collect it. So we had peach ice cream every evening on the front porch. The peaches came from our own trees *[Dad loved peaches – peach pie, peach cobbler, but ice cream, most of all.].* This was after Will died and I think Maggie was down to one cow that year. The next year they sold the farm and moved so Bivon could go to teachers college.

Otherwise Maggie stored food in a cold cellar, under the house, with a dirt floor, which was very dark, but cool. I hated being sent down there to bring something up or to put something down there. It was spooky! But that's why you need a boy on your farm: to run and fetch things for you!

At some farms the perishable food was kept in the springhouse, where the water came up cold from deep underground. The Kinzers had a smokehouse and an outhouse, but no springhouse! There was one farm where Byron Kinzer, who was well-known and well-liked all over the county, was privileged to help himself to a drink of cold buttermilk from their springhouse.

The only dependable income—cash—was Byron's. Bivon would find occasional work as a farmhand, painting barns, or repairing cars. Otherwise, this was truly subsistence farming. Bivon and Byron weren't paid when they worked on the family farm - their pay was a roof over their head and food on the table. This is fine when you are young, but when you get older you'd like a wife and family and a place of your own. And that's what happened: Brooks left, Clara married and left, Will died,...eventually Byron moved on and it was just Maggie and Bivon trying to run a farm together,

Grandmother had another brother, Bayles, (James Bayles Kirk, 1860-1938) who lived in Altoona and worked for the railroad. He owned houses too, and collected rent. The Kirks were all tall good-looking people.

Grandmother had one other brother, Sam, who went to Cleveland and married well. He was a widower and lived next to his daughter Edna, married to Eddie Burchfield, who taught me how to play cribbage. Eddie was a retired railroader. He had a son named Lee from his first marriage. Lee had joined the army due to lack of employment, and served at Schofield Barracks in Honolulu a couple years before the Japanese attacked.

Sam had a sister-in-law, Hally. She owned property in Brown Town the Negro neighborhood in Cleveland. She once offered me a nickel. "You can keep it," she said. I should have framed it; it was probably the only nickel she ever willingly handed over.

How do I know all this? Well, Uncle Sam visited Reeds Gap one summer when I was there. He took to me, his grand-nephew. We went to Columbus, Ohio, together. It was my first journey out of the state; no, it was my second journey.

When I was in second or third grade, my dad and his brother Byron drove to the World's Fair in Chicago and took me along to "A Century of Progress Exposition," the Chicago World's Fair of 1933/34. We drove straight through and found a nice boarding house with meals. It had clean rooms with a nice breeze off lake Michigan every night. We stayed a week, that was my first trip to Chicago!

There was a store in Reeds Gap owned by Earl Harris. It was a real country store. You could buy oats, feed corn, tobacco, rope, barbed wire fencing, nails, all kinds of hardware, thread, buttons, and bolts of cloth. The cloth was pretty to see. I liked the display of thread, with dozens of colors, too.

I could not afford the neat pocket knife I saw at Harris's store. My dad left a dollar for me in nickels, and that was my pocket money for the whole summer.

You could barter with Harris. A huckster would come by and pick up the milk, butter and eggs that Harris had accepted in barter from nearby farmers. The huckster would have things Harris wanted, too, and he would barter or pay cash. Barefoot girls would walk up to the store and trade a dozen eggs for a half pound of butter or some canned milk. And then Harris would trade the eggs for something else.

I didn't like Mr. Earl Harris, the country store owner. I found him disgusting, obese, and selfish. He would slice off fresh pieces of meat and cheese from the supply in his refrigerators and eat them in front of people, showing his delight. These were often people unable to afford that kind of snack. Most people in the country were hungry all the time in those years. It struck me as a very mean thing to do.

I distinctly remember a girl my age staring at him with envy and hunger. She was there to barter a basket of eggs for flour. She was one of Joe Murphy's daughters, who were all good-looking girls.

The bread truck would pull up and what a smell it had! The truck was full of cakes, sticky buns, and fresh bread. They would fill the bread box outside the store with dozens of loaves of bread, and the bread box inside the store too. It smelled so good!

The smells of a country store! There were feed oats, wheat, straw, kerosene, all kinds of dry goods, penny candy, soap … and always the smell of the fresh bread delivered daily—big, heavy, loaves. But also tools and hardware, saws, scythes, rakes, jute rope, rifles and ammunition.

The country smells were unusual to me. Pigs and cows are stinky, but when you mix the carry-over smell with the smell of the smokehouse and the barn, the hay and grass, gasoline, and sweaty overalls the mix becomes an unforgettable and not unpleasant smell. Words fail to describe it.

The smell of a farmer is also worth describing. He was sweaty, but he also smelled of fresh-cut hay from the fields and he would smell like his horse, horses have a nice smell. If it was Saturday, he may have taken a bath and put on freshly-washed and -ironed clothes; nothing fancy, just a blue denim shirt.

Loafers sat outside Harris' store passing the day in idleness. They would talk about local affairs and also listen to whoever had read a newspaper that day. Grandmother Kinzer took a daily newspaper, the *Philadelphia Record*. I liked the comics, especially Tim Tyler's "Luck." That newspaper was just about her only indulgence.

Bruce Woodward (pronounced "Woodert") was one of the regular loafers. He was a dangerous man. Bruce would stop by uninvited; he just showed up. My grandmother feared him even when he was sober. Once in a drunken fit, he struck his son, Rex, with an axe, just below the knee, crippling him for life! That's why he had the reputation he had.

He only visited when she sat on the screened-in front porch, which was delightfully scented by honeysuckle vines, another memorable smell. If you weren't sitting on the porch, Bruce knew you were too busy to be bothered, but woe betide you if you were sitting on the porch and he felt like visiting! I could feel tension in the air then, as Maggie was too polite—or scared—to drive him off.

"Billy E" Woodward was probably a relative. He lived up the dirt road leading to Black Log, in a one-room shake at the foot of the mountain. Tom Woodward lived with him, Tom was a hunchback, a good friend of the Kinzers with a good sense of humor despite his shrunken posture. *[According to his WWII draft registration Tom Woodward was five feet tall, and 100 pounds with a deformed spine.]*

The ugliest person I ever knew was Sam Buchanan. He was about 16 years old and ran a farm with his mother, Em. They shot deer out of season, I was told. The farm was a short distance up the dirt road. Sam never stopped by, but Em did, if my grandmother was sitting out on the porch, a pleasant place to rock. By the way, Buchanan was pronounced "Bah-cannon."

There was a John Buchanan that lived a half-mile up route 36. He was an honest-to-God blacksmith, nicknamed John Buck. He had a brother named Frank who was dying of TB. He would sit on a chair watching John Buck pump the bellows, forge, and hammer on the anvil. He still had an operating forge when I was a boy.

By the thirties, John Buck's stock-in-trade was repairing parts of farm equipment. He was also a good auto mechanic. Automobiles were cheap and changed hands often, A used coupe (front seat only) could be purchased for $25 or $30 cash. John Buck could hammer out the spare part you needed. He was a pleasant man, but so grimy! He had a grimy wife who managed a grimy household. They had a daughter called Punk, ten or eleven years old, who used four-letter words and profanity like a trooper! I do not exaggerate. Grandmother would have no part of them, but Grandfather would go to John Buck for repair work.

[If you look at the 1930 US Census sheets for Tuscarora Township, Juniata County, you can find all these families listed as the neighbors of Will and Maggie Kinzer. Dad's memory was pretty astounding, he rarely slipped. He told me once that starting in his 80s he had these moments of startlingly-clear memories of his childhood: names, faces, and events coming to the surface after decades of lying dormant.]

Grandmother once told me about an arrest. Why she told me makes no sense, because kids do carry tales to others and I'm sure this is one she didn't want repeated. In the 1920s during Prohibition, Byron Kinzer built a still for Bill E. and a couple of his friends. They were raided by the Federals and sentenced to five years in the state penitentiary. They did not squeal on Byron Kinzer. As the builder of the still, he would have been held equally guilty. Maybe they respected his handiwork and looked forward to engaging him again when they got out. Or maybe there was some obscure honor system involved. I never heard this story from anyone else in Reeds Gap.

Yes, kids carry tales from home to others. I overheard Mother saying to someone that Mildred Mackey was "due to have a baby." I was in third grade. When the teacher asked the class if anyone had news to share I raised my hand and announced to the whole class that "Mrs Mackey's going to have a baby!" Sexual matters - and I knew nothing of sex - were taboo in those days and I was soundly rebuked by the teacher, and then again by my mother when I got home!

The men gathered at the store in the evening and they'd pitch horseshoes. Earl Harris's store featured a horseshoe ring with three points for a ringer, two for a leaner, and one point to the shoe nearest the stake. There were single players and teams of two. One tactic was trying to top an opponent's ringer, which was worth six points, or to knock over an opponent's leaner. The game was 21 points.

Pocket money was scarce, but people still managed to have fun. People went to church, which was an event that went on for most of the day. Worshippers came early and greeted each other. Then the service, and after you'd go to Sunday School while the adults would talk and visit some more. You'd be all cleaned up wearing your best clothes, so it was both a church and a social event.

There were festivals on Friday and Saturday evenings. There were all kinds of clubs and associations that people belonged to and they would sponsor a festival, pot-luck, raffle, games and sometimes music and dancing. The ladies would sell ice cream, cakes, cookies, and pies to raise money for various things.

There was a lot of baseball. All the little villages had teams that practiced in any stray field. I was bat boy for the Reeds Gap team. The team would pass the hat during the game to collect pennies and nickels to pay for the bats and balls. They could never beat East Waterford, but usually managed to win over Cross Keys and McConnelsville. The boys owned their own gloves, but the balls and bats were kept for them. Bivon played first base, and Byron was the catcher. He had a chest protector and a mask, which belonged to him.

An ordained preacher was in town every three weeks or so. My grandmother would prepare the Communion service tray when that Sunday arrived. Otherwise, a church elder gave the lesson and led the prayers and singing. Ordinarily there was no Communion, so it was even more important to accept it when you could.

For Reeds Gap there was a movie house in East Waterford that showed silent movies. I went to the movies in Roaring Spring just about every Saturday. The movie house in Roaring Spring would also have prize nights on weeknights, and I recall winning a turkey and having to walk home carrying it, much to the surprise of everyone at home! *[John and Jamie spent several summers with Poppy and Meme when they lived on Poplar Street. Poppy and John went to the Roaring Spring movie house to see "The Guns of Navarone." They both enjoyed the movie very much!]*

Mother would not stay the night in Reeds Gap. She was a town girl, used to running water, electricity, and toilets. She would drive out for the day for a visit or to celebrate a birthday or a holiday, but she would not stay overnight. The stairs up to the second floor were more like a ladder, and there were chamber pots to contend with.

Brooks understood Mother, and doted on her. He liked that she was kind and gentle, generous, and ladylike. He didn't expect her to "climb the wooden mountain" and sleep on a rope bed. But Brooks was quite used to this way of living and I think he wanted me to know about it too - so I wouldn't be soft and spoiled like a city boy.

During the year he would drive out to the country on weekends, taking me with him to deliver groceries, collect funeral insurance payments, and do chores for his Mom. This needed after grandfather had passed and Byron had married. It was just Grandmother and Uncle Bivon living there. Brooks must have been supporting them with groceries and money. Family looked out for each other, you had to.

# GROWING UP IN ROARING SPRING

People like to mention their first memory. Most of my friends won't believe me when I tell them I have a memory from when I was perhaps even less than a year old. I can remember standing on my toes, being held up or dandled, in front of a train window, with my hands and face pressed up against the cold glass, looking out at the land covered in snow. We were traveling backward; that's the other distinct part of the memory. My mother said we lived in Allentown for a while when my father was doing drafting work for the Pennsylvania Railroad, but we left there before I turned three.

Mother feels we were probably riding the train back to Roaring Spring during the winter of 1924-25 or 25-26. The memory of that train ride with my mother is still with me.

How did we get from Roaring Spring to Bethlehem and then back to Roaring Spring?

Dad was trained as a draftsman in Washington DC. With his certificate he was hired by the Pennsylvania Railroad and was assigned a desk job at Allentown in the first years of his marriage. That's where they were newlyweds and that's where we lived when I was born.

My mother went home to Roaring Spring about the time I was due, so she could have Annetta's care. Annetta had 12 children herself, so she would have been a good nurse, especially to her youngest daughter. Mother stayed close to home all her life and she lived to be 94.

I was born at the Nason Hospital on July 10, 1924, at precisely 4:30 in the afternoon. The train from Martinsburg also arrived at the Roaring Spring station at 4:30, and for years afterward I was told that I was delivered to the family by the afternoon train from Martinsburg.

My pediatrician was Dr. Ralph Rhorbaugh. Following his theories, my mother would bundle me in a carriage (she told me) parked on their front porch in winter, even with the snow blowing! I was put out there for my naps; Dr Rohrbaugh believed that cold, fresh air was better for a baby than a stuffy house and overheated air. She was criticized for this: "That little boy will get pneumonia!" or "Lillian Kinzer is nuts!" But she was proud to respond, "Jimmy is a Rohrbaugh baby!"

When I was a small boy, Mother returned to Roaring Spring to help her when her mother was ill. Those were visits, but eventually the return was made permanent. When Annetta died of kidney failure, she left a small household behind: her husband, in his seventies, and dying of prostate cancer, and her son Byron, who was still recovering from his injuries in WW1. There was a woman, Frieda, I think was her name, who did the housework and cooking. After Annetta passed, Mother took over keeping house for my Grandfather. She ran two households.

**Brooks holding Jimmy in the summer of 1924. The photo was taken in the backyard of the Williams home on East Main Street in Roaring Spring during a visit to show off their new baby. Compare Brooks' attire to that of his Father's on the cover of this book to get an idea of how town life compared to country life in the 1920s.**

We moved back to Roaring Spring and lived in a new bungalow not far from the Williams homestead. This was 1927 or

1928. There was a commercial property for sale, down the street from the Methodist church. Brooks prevailed on Grandfather Williams to sign a note for the purchase price. This was when James Shane was still doing well in business and the note was for a five year duration, which he could manage at the time.

Brooks started a grocery store/butcher shop in the largest store space, and collected rent from the other businesses and apartments. It was a good investment, and Brooks' monthly payments to James Shane Williams kept him afloat those last years of his life.

Dad, and a partner named Joe *Something*, I used to know his name, opened a grocery store and meat market. The building included a newsstand/candy store, (run by Galen Snyder,) a corner gas station, a barber shop (Ira Helsel), and four apartments on the second floor. These businesses all did well, and Brooks was able to close-out the loan from Grandfather before he died.

Dad still owned those properties when we moved to Altoona in 1935. The rent paid by Ira Helsel was credited with the haircuts he gave us: 25 cents for me, 50 cents for Dad. While waiting to be next in the chair I would read "Popular Mechanics." While Dad went upstairs to collect the rents on the apartments, I leafed through pulp fiction magazines at Galen Snyder's store. Pulp fiction was sold to the retailers for a nickel a copy, and sold for a dime in the store.

There were punch cards with awards for the winning punch numbers; Galen Snyder featured them at 10 cents a punch, three punches for 25 cents. The numbers were on tightly-coiled paper, and pressed into tiny holes in a board, ten or so across and ten or so in vertical columns. The customer paid and then punched out his choice. Punching opened the coiled paper and gave the number to Galen to record. Brooks won a .300 Savage rifle one time, and that was something—the best prize there was.

Dad discontinued managing the store in Roaring Spring. This was probably 1932 or 1933. He could make more money managing the larger grocery stores owned by the Schafers and then supervising a manager he hired for his own Roaring Spring store. He served as a manager of a Shafer's store in Altoona and another Schafer's store they owned in Martinsburg. So Brooks was collecting rents from the building in Roaring Spring and a salary from the Schafer's.

He used that money to add the small service station to his holdings in Roaring Spring. It was the height of the Depression, but no matter how poor you were you needed gasoline and oil. It wasn't as though Brooks was wealthy but he had small amounts of money coming in from many sources and that made a good living, even with the Great Depression going on all round us.

Verus Stover told Dad of an opening as an agent for Prudential Insurance Company. This would be a step up from managing grocery stores. Dad applied and was accepted. The territory was rural and he enjoyed dealing with country folks. They were simple people and you had to earn their trust. But he was a country boy, too, and people knew the Kinzer name, so he did well.

But eventually he was transferred to Altoona. Sitting at a desk in town was not his cup of tea, but maybe he was tired of Roaring Spring and the Williams family and all their problems.

He stayed with Prudential until his retirement aged 65. He was pensioned moderately. At his retirement dinner he was given a camera, applause, and handshakes. Months later he was in a car accident and the next day, at home, he died of a massive heart attack, toppling over in the living room of the new rambler my parents had moved to a few years before.

The smartest thing Brooks did was purchase a 30 year annuity from Prudential, for Mother. He did this when he turned 60. He had always handled their money and knew she would be too kindly and generous, especially with her family, it was her nature. So an annuity was a good idea, but he had no idea how prescient this decision was. Mother lived for 29 and a half years after he died, and she was well-provided for.

You kids knew that house, the rambler, a sunny and modern house. It was on a big corner lot, with room for a rose garden, a small pool and cherry trees. 900 Poplar street, just outside Roaring Spring proper.

One time Brooks took Barney along with him on his insurance route, which included Morrison's Cove. While driving, the two of them would exchange views as to which farm they would retire to. Barney also got on with Uncle Byron Kinzer, and especially with his beagle pups.

Glass's farm was across the street. They were nice people. They'd see our car with Illinois plates pulled up to the house and they'd call over to mother: "We had a litter of piglets two days ago, there's plenty for you grandkids to hold if you send them over." That kind of thing. Ralph Glass taught young Barney how to call pigs. Soooo-wee!

You kids were invited over to Glass's farm to see two calves that were born. Snippy went with you, she liked seeing baby animals too. One calf was still in the barn but the older calf, a day or two old, was out in the pen with the other cows. One cow was bothering the new calf, still fragile and shaking. You kids called your mom, who came straight out of the barn to see what the problem was. Snippy always hated a bully and she climbed right through that fence and started batting and shoving the cow! Well, none of you expected that to happen, and now you kids were scared for your mother! You hollered at your mom to get back on the safe side of the fence and one of Glass' hands heard you and came running too!

The Kettners lived next door to Poppy and Meme. Due to a quarrel with the Kettner kids, Jamie and Barney retaliated with a mud bombardment to the side of the Kettners' house. Jim was too smart to get involved, but Jamie was a hothead, and little Barney was her dupe. Dottie Kettner complained to my mother, who was a good teaser.

That night at the dinner table, she read aloud an interesting news story from the evening paper: the police were looking for suspects in a damaging mud-throwing incident!

Jamie was sure Meme was making it up and challenged her, but Meme just kept "reading" the news story about the mud throwing and the ongoing investigation by the police.

When I was a boy I was abandoned on a road trip. We stopped at a restaurant on a road trip to Akron, Ohio, to visit Meme's sister Clara and her husband, Uncle Frank McDermott. I ate little and went to the magazine rack to leaf through the comic books. The folks forgot about me, loaded up the car and left. Uncle Hon was along too. After driving for a bit, someone said "Where's Jimmy!" They turned around and found me still reading comic books. I had not missed them and all their chatter for one minute.

Frank McDermott had a nice job as a supervisor for Firestone in Akron. It was a good paying job, but he risked his employment by siding with the Firestone strikers, serving as a sort of quartermaster by furnishing the strikers with cots to sleep on. It was poor judgment on Frank's part, and disloyal, for he enjoyed the benefits of a Firestone manager while giving aid to those strikers. The split between his actions and what was right wasn't something I understood, but I felt it strongly. I had no one to discuss these thoughts with, because as far as I knew, there were no Republican voters in my family.

My childhood was full of experiences, I think because I was part of such a large family. I had all those living aunts and uncles on my mother's side and two more uncles and an aunt on my father's side. In a small town like Roaring Spring (3,000 souls), friendships and acquaintances spread like ripples on a pond.

In Reeds Gap people lived further apart but the connections were much stronger there, and I was always hearing about the Kirks, the Murphys, and the Lauvers.

Going home from school one day, I was stopped by a man in a parked car. He had a bag full of magazines: *Saturday Evening Post, Ladies Home Journal* and *Country Gentleman.* "Sell these at ten cents a copy. I'll be here next week to collect the money and pay you three cents for each copy you sell." Done! But I sold none. He moved on to who knows where, an itinerant hoping to make a dollar a week.

There was an itinerant music teacher who knocked at the front door offering to loan us an instrument while you paid for lessons: violin, guitar or banjo. Offer accepted, and a pledge signed; guitar was my choice. But his tour of Roaring Spring produced no additional takers. He picked up the guitar a day later and went on his way.

It seemed like everyone was looking for the next dollar, and the next meal. Being rootless and without a home, was about the worst thing that could happen to you.

There was hardly any crime, but Roaring Spring had a good one when "Pickle" Huston and a friend robbed a hardware store on Main Street, across from the newsstand where I leafed through pulp magazines (10 cents a copy) like *Detective Special, G-8 and his Flying Aces,* and *Texas Round-up.* "Pickle" Huston and his fellow robber left the hardware store in a shambles. They were looking for guns and ammunition. When the owner saw the destruction the following morning he dropped dead on the spot, and that's the truth! They got twenty years in the State Penitentiary at Huntington.

Oh yes, there was another involving embezzlement by Mr. Bassler, who had charge of county funds. He went to jail in the County prison in Hollidaysburg, which was an immense limestone edifice like a medieval fortress; that awed me. I would only glance at it from the corner of my eye, and ditto that for the penitentiary at Huntingdon, which we passed when driving to Reeds Gap.

There were two Bassler boys. One was named "Merk." His brother, Clayton, went on to Penn State (probably on scholarship) where I met him after the war. I never heard what happened to "Merk," except that he went on to Texas.

I was approached one day in 1932 by a man I knew, but now I forget his name. "Here are some pets from the hunting club you can have, Jimmy." I was enthralled! There was a tame raccoon, a great horned owl, and two squirrels! One was a so-called flying squirrel with webs between its toes like parachutes. No one was happy about this at home. The animals, though tame, were not actually pets. They were messy and had to be fed and watered.

Byron Kinzer came up from Reeds Gap to get them, but one of those creatures was nearly the death of me. My symptoms were enlargements of the lymph nodes in the groin and under the armpit, which rendered me a cripple. Dad had to carry me up and down the stairs, drive me to school and carry me into the classroom. This lasted at least a month.

Local doctors had no diagnosis, let alone a cure. A chiropractor was tried, but he was no help. It was probably due to good natural health that I eventually recovered, thanks also to my mother, who went by the book raising me. Dr. John Kinzer thinks I had Lyme disease, *or maybe even the Plague!*

Mae Shoeman lived on East Main Street in Roaring Spring, across from my grandparents. I was almost like her adopted child. I called her "Shoeman" and she thought that was funny. Her husband, Charlie, had a steady job at the railyard roundhouse in Altoona. He was never out of work in the Depression, so he must have been a good foreman. His right arm was tattooed with a corseted lady in pink tights.

That whole family virtually adopted me. Shoeman had a son, Paul Snyder, from her first marriage.

She had another son, Fred, who died of tuberculosis in 1927 or 28, They had a daughter named Bernadine. Would you believe she took me to bed with her until I was six? She bathed me first. She had a picture of Clark Gable on the nightstand next to her bed. Paul teased her about that. She tried to be a school teacher but failed at it, because as Shoeman said, "She couldn't keep order."

Paul was still living at home when I was a frequent guest, and I remember reporting to his mother, "Paul is smoking in bed, Shoeman!"

She was a great cook, especially pies and cakes; she always gave me the bowl and spoon to lick. Elderberry pie was my favorite. We picked the berries from bushes at the top of the road. The stem was held in the left hand and you carefully stripped off the berries with the finger tip of your right hand, so as not to crush them. I wasn't of much use, but I was made to feel otherwise. At Shoeman's I was allowed to wash down my pie with a cup of coffee, which made my mother cringe.

At the kitchen table I sat next to Bernadine. Charlie was to my left, at the head of the table. Shoeman was to my right at the other end, and Paul sat opposite. Why do I tell you all this in such detail? Only so you will know how welcome I was, a puny kid too young to go to school.

The Shoeman's had a good radio at their house, a Philco. I listened to nearly all the 15 minute episodes of Orphan Annie, but I never got an Orphan Annie decoder ring. With its decoding ability, you were supposed to get a secret message and a report about things to come.

Shoeman said to me one day, "Jimmy, so many programs every day bother me. Pick two, and that's enough." It was a hard choice. There was Jack Armstrong, All-American Boy, Orphan Annie, Tom Mix, the Ralston Roundup, and Inspector Post.

I maintained a friendship and closeness with the Shoemans. After my parents moved from Roaring Spring to Altoona, I was homesick for them and would often hitchhike back to Roaring Spring. When I did, I would always spend the night with the Shoemans. Once I was picked up by a man who asked me where I was going. I told him

I was going to see Paul Snyder. This had to be Christmas of 1936 or '37, and I was maybe 12. My patron said "Ah, Paul and I once undressed a woman in a car." I had no response to that!

Paul Snyder was a very successful salesman for Colgate-Palmolive-Peet; he traveled to Roanoke, Kansas City, Boise, and Wyoming. He bought boxes of Colgate products home at Christmastime. He had neither health insurance nor a retirement benefit, but he made good money and was generous.

Paul must have been a natural at selling, even though, as he told me, he never made it past seventh grade. He was tall, good-looking, always immaculately dressed and groomed, an impressive looking man. He drove a Cadillac.

If Paul was home for Christmas he would take me shopping in Altoona, and always suggested I get perfumed bath salts for his wife, Jacqueline; he paid for it too. She was his second wife. His first marriage had ended in divorce.

When we went on our annual shopping expedition, we'd stop first at "Bull" Snyder's bar for the purpose of "... a little Christmas Cheer, Jimmy, before we go on about our business!"

Next, in Altoona, there was a mystery stop. Paul would visit someone for nearly an hour while I sat in the car parked well down the street, reading a magazine that Paul had just bought for me. *Who was he visiting and why the one- hour stop?*

He had syphilis, and it was killing him. He had no health insurance and it was a death sentence. Paul applied to my Dad, who was an agent for Prudential by then. The doctor turned him down; he detected the syphilis of course, and he had a bad heart already. I was 10 or 11, and Dad said to me, "Do you know what's wrong with Paul?" I don't know how I knew, but I did. Maybe I had put two and two together.

Three others had died of syphilis in Roaring Spring, a thing not mentioned by name, and never presented its full meaning to me. I amaze myself to recall so well a tragedy of sinful behavior in Roaring Spring, doubtless because I didn't understand the cause, but sensed the tragedy, nonetheless. Altoona was only 15 miles away and young men were tempted by the experiences of others before them.

Four of the young men of Roaring Spring died of the worst venereal disease: Paul S., Frank B., John H. and my uncle, Ross Williams. I think the four of them were likely infected by the same woman in Altoona. I did not know my uncle Ross Williams. He was rarely spoken of. My grandfather sent him to Arizona to die, out of shame for the whole family, of course.

Frank B. was a dentist. He had an office on the third floor of the bank building, but because of his bad heart he had to move his practice to his home on East Main St. He died of heart disease. John H. was a barber at Roy Green's barber shop. He had a peculiar posture and a silly crooked grin. He lived with his sister, a nurse at Nason Hospital. At noon, I once saw her trudging home, disconsolate, to take care of her brother John in his last days. I was told he died an idiot.

That may have been Paul's fate, too. Because of his declining health, Colgate fired him some time in the 1940s. Shoeman died of cancer just after I came home from the war, in 1945. I went to her funeral and that was the last time I saw Paul and Jacqueline. He truly loved his mother and could not stand to return to town with her gone.

I kept up with Paul and his wife Jacqueline. For a time they had a bar in Kansas City, part of his former territory when he was a salesman. Then they lived together in Virginia, in a house she had inherited. The good times were over and they were broke.

Paul and I exchanged a few letters when I was in law school at George Washington University, so even at that late date he was alert and could write. When I suggested I visit them, Paul wrote back declining, saying he would probably just break down. He was in the last stages by then.

As a kid of eleven or twelve years old, you can imagine what it meant to me to figure out that men I knew so well in Roaring Spring had died of syphilis, though my understanding was hazy. Elsie Esper, my Altoona Sunday School teacher, once paused in a lesson to remark "There are diseases people get when they sin." And that was about as close as any adult ever got to explaining it to me.

The deprivations of the Great Depression were very real in towns and cities, but the farm folk were used to hard times. Children went barefoot for as long as they could during the summer and into the fall, shoes being about the only thing you couldn't mend and hand down. And shoes cost money. Mostly, you bartered for what you could. A lot of things cost a nickel a pound, like bananas. Other things were a dime: a loaf of bread, a pack of cigarettes, a gallon of gas.

The unemployed, hobos, would stop by in Roaring Spring, but not Reeds Gap. I guess they knew the country folk didn't have much to share. They would be on the road and they would come to the backdoor, take their hat off, and tell their story of woe. My mother, Lillian, would give them a hot meal: they ate sitting on the back porch and thanked you afterwards. You didn't invite them in, and they stood back because they didn't expect to be invited in. They were polite and respectful.

The beggars stopped at Mae Shoeman's house, too. She didn't invite the beggars in either, but always gave them a good meal to eat on her stoop.

This reminds me of a story from the Walnut Street house period. For some reason I had to be scolded and sought comfort for myself, lying under the back porch for hours. I always took criticism poorly. This was the year of the Lindbergh baby kidnapping and I was 7 or 8. Mother called around and Father searched Roaring Spring in an effort to find me. Eventually I got tired of being under the porch and came out. Later I heard him laughing it off. "We had no idea what happened to him until he showed up for dinner!"

At about this same time, when Dad was managing stores for Shafer's, they took "Relief Orders" and provided staples for the indigent. Brooks had a helper who drove a Ford pickup truck and I was a sometime passenger. I can remember being seven or eight, riding in the truck to deliver a couple boxes of groceries, a relief to a family in what they called the Barrens in Blair County, just outside Martinsburg. This was where my Williams uncles, Carl and Byron, and their friends Johnny "Mutt" Bowers and Steve Sell hunted rabbits. They would take me with them so I knew the area.

We carried the groceries in and unpacked the large boxes on the kitchen table. The women's five children came in and watched as each item came out of the boxes. They didn't say a word. They just stood and watched the food come out, thinking their own thoughts. I felt sorry for them and embarrassed by their silence and their disbelief as bags were opened and the contents were spread across their kitchen table.

I was probably a little ashamed of my own good fortune. Not that my family was wealthy; we just didn't want for things.

Our first car was an Essex. The rear axle broke so often Dad carried a spare one in the trunk. It was a handsome car, but unfortunately, an unreliable one.

In 1937, when I was 13 and we lived in Altoona, my allowance was a quarter. I didn't know how lucky I was. That paid for a movie, ten cents, and a bag of candy for the movie, with five cents, and ten cents leftover to buy a stamp for my stamp collection. Movies were a great treat, an unbelievable deal. I'd see a double feature, and cartoons, a newsreel, a comedy short and an episode of an adventure serial! The serials left me hanging from week to week. You'd think your hero was a goner, but the next Saturday I'd find out I'd been fooled and the hero had escaped through some ridiculous and unbelievable turn of events.

Joe Black had the movie house franchise in Roaring Spring, and owned the property where the theater was located. He operated a bowling alley and pool room, too. "Friday" Bowers was the projectionist. Mother once told me that Brooks lost $20 to a pool shark, which was a lot of money in the 1920s. Attendance at movies was forbidden by the Church of God and to the foot-washing brethren, but my mother, usually so worried about "what people would think!" allowed me to watch any movie I wanted.

Mother was fond of playing bridge with her girlfriends. Cards were also forbidden by the Methodists, so I guess Mother understood my desire to go to the movies.

On Valentine's Day cards were exchanged in grade school, carried from home. My mother supervised the list in third grade (Miss Treese) and she challenged me. "Where is the card for Helen Weitzel?" Helen Weitzel was ugly and I had not set one aside for her. "You're giving her one," my mother commanded, which I did, and was teased about it afterward by all the other boys.

I attended four grades in Roaring Spring. First grade was Miss Martin. Second grade was Emma Bolger. Third grade was Miss Trease. The fourth grade teacher I don't remember. That was when my jaw was healing from the car accident with my mother.

The teachers read stories to us. When it was the Bobsey Twins, we boys groaned. When it was the Rover Boys, the girls groaned.

Halloween was a party day at school, a big deal and a day we looked forward to as much as Christmas. We came to school in disguise, dressed as characters. My mother and her friend, Mid Mackey, dressed me as Little Red Riding Hood in Mrs Mackey's kitchen. I had a red cloak, girls' shoes, girls' frilly socks, a girl's hat and a mask. I was told, "Don't say a word, Jimmy, just shake your head when they think they've guessed your name." No one ever guessed who I was, so I stood alone by the end of the contest. This was second grade, I believe. No one expected a boy to be dressed as Little Red Riding Hood. The prize was a volume of *Bomba the Jungle Boy!*

A neighbor woman named Clara Ebersole made pocket money during the Depression by selling her homemade cookies door-to-door. They were terrible cookies, and known everywhere as Clara's Burnt Leather Cookies. But people bought them anyway, out of kindness.

There is also the story about another neighbor, Thelma Thompson. She wasn't "all there." Lillian left her in charge of me and my little sister, Jo Ann, while she went to take care of her dying father. Mother was away and Thelma was watching us. Thelma decided she was going to kill Jo Ann and me, and started chasing us around the dining room table with a butcher's knife shouting, "I'm going to kill you kids!"

I sent Jo Ann to get Mother and ran in a diverting direction. Thelma followed me and Jo Ann made it out of the house. I shouted to Jo Anne "Go get Mother! I'll keep her chasing me until you get back with Mother." I remember those words distinctly. I can't remember exactly how all it ended, but Thelma eventually went to the funny farm. This would have been around 1931 when we lived in a nice new house, a modern Bungalow, on Walnut Street.

Uncle Carl's family had it tough during the Depression. Carl was called "Hun" by everyone, short for Honey. He was the baby in my mother's family, and his oldest brothers and sisters were about grown when he showed up. They carried him everywhere, even when he was so big it started to look a little silly. Baby Honey became Uncle Hun.

He was married to a fine woman, Hazel. Aunt Hazel, little as she was, was the one who kept things going. Carl had work as a bakery truck driver and as a store clerk, but work was scarce and the hours might be few. During the Depression, Hazel roasted peanuts, made candy, and also did handcrafts. Her children sold them door-to-door. There is always a market for something tasty or pretty.

The children were Betty Jean, Joyce, Diana, and young Carl (Betty Jean and Joyce were about Dad's age.) Young Carl became a Methodist minister. Betty Jean went to nursing school. Then she put Joyce through school, and then Joyce put Diane through school. Then Diane put young Carl through Divinity school. They have all done well.

Their father did odd jobs. One was driving a bakery truck through neighborhoods, selling bread door-to-door. I did this with him even though I was a little kid. The inside of the truck smelled so good! Everything came right out of the oven and went into the truck for sale, still warm. I can remember going to the backdoors and calling out "Brea-ea-ead!" The lady would then come to the door and tell me what she wanted from the truck and I'd go fetch it and make change.

When World War II came on, men at home were scarce. My Dad, with Prudential, got Hazel Williams a job as a Prudential agent in rural Blair County. One day, while making her rounds, she struck a jay-walking cow with her car. The farmer complained that the cow gave no milk after the accident. That was his claim. Who was responsible: was it jaywalker Bess or was it careless Hazel? That was the joke around town. Prudential compensated for the unresponsive udder.

Aunt Hazel was fond of me. When I went off to war, she gave me a small New Testament with steel covers, which I was to wear close to my heart. Well, bless her.

Carl and Hazel were not the only ones to struggle through the Depression. You have no idea how families moved about and changed jobs in order to find income. Situations were dire. The Hamers were unsuccessful with a bakery in Roaring Spring and left for Altoona. The MacMillans were neighbors on Walnut Street, and they left. I remember another family that lived a block from us in Altoona, then moved to New Jersey. Ed Williams lost a good job in Altoona and moved with his wife Alfaretta for a not-as-good job in Pittsburgh. He was an engineer and the new job paid poorly, but there was a paycheck.

Being homeless and on the road. I think that's about the worst thing that can happen to a man…but to have it happen to your whole family is far worse. We humans are meant to have an identity and a home, connections, a place that is our's. The bad economy stole that from many people.

So that covers George, Ross, Merrill, Paul, Byron, Ed, Glen, and Carl Williams. My mother also had three sisters. Ruth Susan and Bessie Celestia both died as children when Mother was still a baby. Clara, her only other sister, moved away when she married. Clara had a bad heart and died in 1952.

Mother died in 1994, aged 94. The last of her generation. She was sitting up and reading her Bible when she passed.

In Roaring Spring I had my first experience of the effects of too much booze. Coming home from a movie one night, I passed a man near the Methodist Church, yorking his guts out. I asked him if he needed help, which only resulted in another big heave.

Palmer McGee owned and operated a dairy. I was sent there one day by Shoeman to buy a quart of milk, and found him staring at me bleary-eyed with a bottle of booze in his hand. McGee had the habit of going missing for months at a time and being brought home from as far away as California. The dairy nonetheless was profitable, thanks to his wife. They had a nice home. There were two children, Palmer Jr., who went to West Point, and Donal, who became a physician.

Before we lived on Walnut St, I remember living, or maybe we were just staying, in the Williams' home. That house was built for them and it was large, well, they'd had 12 children, and it was built by J.A.J. Williams, one of the many houses he built on the Main street. This was where my mother was born and grew up. Through the teens and twenties that house full - until you married or had a good career like Marrill, you lived at home with your parents. None of this renting an apartment as soon as you got your first job. You stayed close to your family.

I have only a few memories of that house. It was big, with many bedrooms and bathrooms. There was a stained glass window on the stair landing, a big front porch with steep steps going straight up from the Main Street.

I remember my grandmother Williams, born Annetta Mauk, rocking me in her chair. Holding me in her lap she'd flip out her false teeth, much to my amazement, chuckling as she did it. I was in her left arm staring at the performance, "Do it again, Gramma!" I think this occurred no later than 1927, because I remember the whole family, all three generations, thrilled over Lindbergh's solo flight across the Atlantic Ocean to Paris. We listened to their radio and read about it in the paper. It caused quite a sensation! Annetta died in 1930.

The "underworld" was also mentioned on the radio a lot at this time, and I remember wondering what it could be like: another world under Roaring Spring? I remember listening to the Jack Dempsey/Jack Sharkey fight *[this was 1927, and a legendary fight. Dad would have been three. Dad's early memories are remarkable.]*

My grandfather Williams died in 1932. He was an accountant with an office at the blank book factory. I saw him one day through a ground floor window, sitting at his desk. At Christmastime, all his children present got $20 gold pieces. The grandchildren, like myself, got a $5 gold piece. He went among us on Christmas day passing them out.

At the time, in 1930 or 1931, we lived on Walnut Street in a nice home my grandfather bought for my mother, who had nursed Annetta for several years. Mother was now looking after Grandfather while he was dying of prostate cancer. When we moved to Walnut Street we acquired a radio that sat on the sun porch overlooking the backyard, where the cesspool had been dug. There was no central sewer system then.

I had many cousins in Roaring Spring. Carl and Hazel had four children, Byron had two, Glenn had two. There were two boy cousins once removed—the children of Jesse Williams, James Shane Williams' younger brother. His boys, Augustus and John were about my age, though their father was a generation older. They were both crippled, with their spines bending a little more each year. They were taught watch repair.

Some of these stories might be boring. But time is passing and one story leads to another.

Roaring Spring had a diphtheria epidemic when I was in grade school. Six or seven children died in 1933 of diphtheria—that's a lot for a small town. Emory Bowers was one who died; he was a school chum of mine.

He came from a poor family; they didn't have a house, they lived in one of the apartments my Father owned. I remember he followed me home one day and as we got close to my house I turned around and said to him "Now, Emory, you can't come home with me. My mother doesn't want me playing with you." That was a cruel thing to say, but it was a fact that my mother didn't want me to play with him.

His cousin, John Bowers, also died from diphtheria. [I confirmed this; both boys died of diphtheria in late 1933. Also, it looks as though Emory's parents were separated at the time, which makes it all the sadder. As dad mentioned, many families were separated or made homeless by the Great Depression.]

Childhood diseases were common and many. I had most, including mumps and measles. The diphtheria deaths were sad; there was a vaccine, but no one in our small town was vaccinated, I guess.

Up until I went away to college we lived in Altoona. We moved to Altoona in 1934. The original plan had been to move to Bedford, but Mother was badly injured in an automobile accident just before that move was made, delaying our move. My jaw was broken in the same accident.

The transfer to Bedford became a transfer to Altoona, a few months later than scheduled, after mother recovered. Dad was now with Prudential. We moved just as I was beginning fifth grade. Altoona was a real city with good schools and a high school that ranked among the best in Pennsylvania.

My weekdays were occupied by school. Saturday was a "day off," and I would spend it playing with other boys, having adventures, or going to the movies.

On a Friday evening I sometimes went to Roaring Spring with my Dad. He would collect his rents and I would spend the night at Shoeman's house, with Mae, Charlie and Bernadine. On some Fridays I would hitchhike to Roaring Spring to visit with friends my own age, and again I would stay the night with the Shoemans. My mother would call ahead to make sure this was okay with Mae Shoeman, and it was always okay!

Sunday we went to church, either in Roaring Spring or in Altoona. In good weather there would be church picnics or ball games. In the winter there was sledding and skating.

I wasn't close to my little sister, Jo Ann. She was four years younger than me and we didn't do much together. Gary, my younger brother, was born when I was 14 so we didn't do much together, either. Mother was Rh-negative, and miscarried several times before Gary was born. I operated more as an "only child," I guess.

At first, Altoona was difficult for me. It was a miserable move. As the new kid, I had to fight Ralph Watson when he purposely tramped on my overshoes, following right behind me on my way to fifth grade at Baker School. The teacher was Marjorie Gaffius, a Scot name. She was very good looking, with a fine, fitting figure. She had a boyfriend who came by the classroom once in a while. His name was Marc something-or-other.

The teachers (fifth and sixth grade) were Clara Cockerill and Marjorie Gaffius. The principal was Miss Clara Bridenstein.

Ralph Watson was a plague until I finally decked him. But I had to beat him up a second time. Mr Pannebacker broke up that fight. Another school-boy fight was with Sam Wilson inside our garage. Jo Ann ran in the house screaming, "Sammy Wilson is killing Jimmy!" I survived, of course. My mother laughed when she told Dad about it that evening.

I liked school, the courses were more challenging. and I did well. I joined Troop 2 and rose rapidly to Eagle Scout.

The Boy Scouts, Troop 2, had a meeting room in Baker School. I joined in the fall when I was twelve years old. The Boy Scouts had a considerable influence on my life, notably through Bob Welker, who was a Harvard student. Bob was very intelligent and a devoted scouter. I became an enthusiastic ornithologist through his influence. We had many bird trips together, particularly at Camp Schaffer, near Huntington, along the Raystown branch of the Juniata River. It was there that I saw my first Maryland Yellow Throat, and heard it's sorry "t'witchy witchy witchy witch." I can still whistle it.

Bob Welker was an atheist and a socialist, often arguing with Bob Bolger, who pitched for the Altoona High School baseball team, and then for Penn State.

The grade school was Baker School, junior high was Roosevelt. [Both were still standing when we last visited, as is the lovely brick bungalow with an extra lot on Browning Avenue Brooks bought for his family to live in.] I recall little more about Baker or Roosevelt, except for three bright girls: Mary Holtzinger, Anne Wertz, and Bonnie Silknetler. No outstanding boys.

I entered Roosevelt Junior High in 1937, three years of it, which I hated. I opted for science there (for yeoman students) not Latin (for aristocratic students.) The difference in class status was well-known. In junior high there were clubs. I needed a merit badge for cooking, and my eyes popped when I saw "camp cooking" as one of the clubs. It wasn't camp cooking at all! It was rudimentary household cooking - cookies, biscuits, jams - I know because I elected to take that class and was the only boy.

**Dad was the quarterback for the "Suicide Squad"**

Altoona High School was a three-year program: sophomore, junior, senior. I excelled in all my classes. For once I was being taught things that really mattered to me: sines and cosines, the binomial theorem, classic English and American writing, vacuums, levers, atoms, and molecules. For me, high school was an exciting adventure. There was a new adventure every day. I have always liked learning, and I think you kids all have that same bug. There's a lot of joy to be had from understanding how things work, or why things are the way they are.

Altoona High was staffed with excellent teachers. I could hardly wait to get there in the morning, a good mile-and-a-half away. I could take a street car for seven cents, or Dad would drive me as he had done all through junior high. The three Demhart kids went along with us, Bernie, Patty, and her twin sister, Marilyn.

I was scarcely big enough to play football, but I was determined to try out for it. I did manage to play footbal, but on the "suicide squad."

The varsity coach was Ken Bashore, assisted by "Sis" Dinges, who had played college football. The junior varsity coaches were Hugh Black and Paul Morris. I washed out from varsity team selection, so I tried for the JVs. Another failed effort. I sat disconsolately on one of the bleacher seats. Ken Bashear and Frank McDermott passed by. Frank looked at me and said to Coach Bashear, "Do you know who that boy is?" "No." He's "Shorty Williams' nephew." I was promptly given a uniform for the JV squad as an up-and-coming quarterback.

In my senior year I was promoted to varsity suicide squad, getting into the game whenever AHS was well ahead. We were taught the T formation, which replaced the single-wing formation. Once I nearly returned a kick-off for a touchdown. That was my only claim to fame as an "up-and-coming" quarterback.

Bashmore stopped me in the hall one day and said, "Kinzer, with your grade point average, two inches and twenty more pounds on you, I could get you in any college, tuition free."

I fell in love several times: Lousie Holzinger, Marjorie Shaw, and Sally Humer. Sally Humer, unknown to me (and her), was a first cousin once removed. Our parents were distraught over the affair. Her mother, Grace, was first cousin to my mother. Her dad's name was "Igat!" Her older sister had been Penn State Homecoming Queen, which was quite something. Well, the adolescent affair with Sally broke up, of course, but I really did love that girl.

I rebelled, but soon fell in love with Marjorie Shaw, who was cute, and chemistry was her favorite class, which is how we met. We'd get together after hours, when we were doing extra credit for chemistry class. After the war, I decided she wasn't good enough for me.

Oh, and Louise Holzinger, but she didn't prefer me, which I concluded after about six years. Our families were close and worshiped together at Llyswen Methodist Church in Altoona. I also suspect that her mother considered the Holtzingers above the Kinzers. Just as well, for Louise was a horsewoman. I have known three horsewomen and they were all tribulations. Besides, she was always sick, and her brother told me Louise needed to marry a wealthy man who could pay for her doctors and horses. Horsewomen are to be avoided, but saying that at the time caused me great embarrassment.

I was far, far from being romantic, and twice failed to realize that I was being plainly seduced by two girls who asked me to walk them home, knowing that their mothers were not there. I didn't even try a kiss! "Faint heart, fair hand never won," and that was me.

One girl was named Elma and the other was Gloria. The prettiest girl was Georgette Miller. She was a true strawberry blonde, a friend to Sally Grimshaw, who depended on me to get her through plane geometry. Sally was a very pretty brunette, well- endowed. Her father, Fred Grimshaw, was the works manager for the PARR shops in Altoona, a very responsible position. She had equally pretty sisters: Jane, Ann, "Tibby," and Marcie. Her brother, Fred, was killed in a pilot training accident early in the war. I liked Sally, but I was not in love with her, nor she with me. We were pals.

Sally's sister, Tibby, was married to Paul Morris, a high school phys ed teacher who taught health. He was a tyrant on the gym floor, but I had no trouble with or from him. A friend of mine, Jim Peters, was a good gymnast on the gym team, which I envied. He had a falling out with Paul Morris, who assigned Jim to the role of Cinderella in the Memorial Day parade. Jim refused to dress as Cinderella and was kicked off the team.

Paul Morris became persona non grata in the Grimshaw family when he took up with a teenage Italian during the war years. I was virtually adopted by the Grimshaw family and spent many a Sunday dinner with the whole family after the war.

My best friend in High School was Russel Alvis. We played football together and went off to college at Penn State together. Penn State had a single campus of about 5,000 students.

The Alvises, Russ' parents, moved to State College when Russ and I went there together. I boarded with them for a few months before I pledged Alpha Chi Sigma. They wanted me as a companion to their only child, believing I would be a good influence on his study habits. He was also enrolled in chemical engineering. Unfortunately, Russ pledged Phi Beta Kappa, his downfall. There was more fun to be had as a Fraternity Rat, and that's the direction Russ went in.

**Dad's 1942 Altoona High School yearbook photo.**

There were more than a few arguments between Russ and his father concerning the empty chair at his study desk next to mine. I was always a good student, loved learning, studied hard and got good grades. I joined a more academic fraternity, which was a good thing. I was a bit of a smart aleck, and fraternity life knocked that out of me.

It was Bob Bolger who reported me to customs at Penn State for not wearing my freshman cap. That caused me much trouble. I was sentenced by tribunal to ring a bell as I moved from class to class, and to wear a sandwich placard that read:

*Jimmie Kinzer is my name.*
*That's my only claim to fame.*
*WEAR CUSTOMS ALWAYS.*

It was then that I pledged Alpha Sigma Chi, limited to chemistry majors. Because of my sentence, I had to enter the fraternity by way of the coal chute. I joined the fraternity through the auspices of a senior chemical engineer, Leonard Fresco. He gave us a lecture and orientation one evening and when he learned I was from Altoona High School and a nephew of George Williams, those credentials amounted to a home run.

**Lt. Kinzer c. 1944**

I enlisted in the Army Air Force and waited to be called up. I went to Nashville, Tennessee by train, where there was a classification center. I took IQ tests, physical tests, aptitude tests and personality tests, all meant to screen out those who weren't qualified to be a pilot, bombardier, or navigator.

I chose to be a navigator. I wouldn't have made a good pilot. I have a maverick attitude and I don't like abiding by rules. A pilot has to follow precise flight discipline and instrument readings. Mathematics and the precision work for navigation with equations and numbers didn't bother me at all. It suited me and it appealed to my strengths: mathematics and science.

When I was interviewed in Nashville, Tennessee as a volunteer for the Air Corps, one of the interrogators asked me if I remembered him. I did not. He smiled and said he was a member of the tribunal at Penn State that sentenced me to wear a penitent verse, and it was he who wrote the mocking verse.

There were two other chance encounters during my service. Russel Alvis left Penn State several months before I did. I briefly saw him marching by one day in Nashville, which was a clearance center and not the pilot school. So he had washed out of pilot school. Everyone wanted to be a pilot, and the Army Air Force set a high standard for their pilots. Many started, but few graduated.

Russel went MIA in December 1944, a gunner on a B-19, when the 8th Air Force was called upon to stem the German advances in the Ardennes Forest thrust, the Battle of the Bulge.

I played bridge with the Alvises after the war, and I sensed there was trouble between them. (My bridge partner was Madge Finkbeiner.) His poor parents, who I knew so well. Russ was their only child, they had even followed him off to State College! Russ was the glue in that marriage, and I'm afraid his death spelled a disaster for them. *[Russ was a very handsome boy in his High School graduation photo: dark hair, square-jawed, dimpled chin, and blue eyes.]*

The other chance encounter was in Marrakesh, Morocco, in 1944. I bumped into David Longennecker of Roaring Spring. He was an enlisted man stationed there.

I was given some preliminary flight training in Nashville, and then I was sent to Buckingham Army Airfield in Ft. Myers, Florida for gunnery school. This was the summer of 1943.

In Florida I got to see so many of the birds in my field guide, birds I never thought I would ever get to see. Even on the train down to the base I was spotting exotic tropical birds. It was very exciting for me to add these birds to my life list. Even though I had the most gawd-awful case of prickly-heat the whole time I was there, the uniforms, I think. I have enjoyed birding, it was just about my favorite Boy Scout badge. But birding in Pennsylvania -or- birding in Florida? There is no comparison!

Any air crew member except the pilots had to be able to handle a 50 caliber machine gun. We learned to strip it down and rebuild it while blindfolded. This I could do, but I was never a good shot with a machine gun and barely passed. I think they moved me forward in my training because they needed navigators more than they needed machine-gun operators, a humiliation for me.

We had a lot of training with rifles, shotguns and sidearms as well. We did have some training in the air, shooting at targets towed over the Gulf of Mexico behind a single wing plane. I suspect those pilots hated that job.

All copilots on B-17s were pulled out of other assignments, the assignments they had chosen. The first pilot was the guy who had asked to pilot B-17s. Our co-pilot, Bernie Jacobs, was pulled from a fighter squadron and assigned to B-17s, distinguished from the F because the G had a nose turret operated by the bombardier. The casualty rate in the army air force was 55% in training and 45% in combat.

Then I was sent to Monroe, Louisiana, for navigator school. There I was the perfect student! When I graduated I got two weeks leave so I went back to Altoona. Then I reported to Rattlesnake Army Airfield in Pyote, Texas. There was a train station, barber shop, service station and a grocery store. That was it. It was there that crews were given their brand new B-17s. We calibrated all the instruments, learned to work together as a crew and ultimately flew that plane to Grand Island, Nebraska where we joined up with a bunch of B-17 crews all ready to fly to Europe.

Our first pilot was Jim MacFarland from Ogden, Utah. He died when he was 55 years old. Our co-pilot was Bernie Jacobs from California, a protestant despite his name. Our engineer was Walter Doughty from Texas, and our radio operator was George Shepherd from Ohio, the oldest of our crew, maybe 30 or 35 years old. Our ball turret was a little guy named Eldon Martin. He had to be small to squeeze into that little shell. The bombardier was Pete Ziegler from Wyoming. Our waist gunner was Frank LaTourette. I had some correspondence from him. He stayed in the Air Corps, finally discharged as a major. I say, "Good for him!" The tail gunner was also older; his name was Carlisle Telford from California. He was killed in a raid on Germany while flying with another crew. Pete Ziegler, assigned to another crew while in combat, bailed out with others from his B-17, and survived the war hiding in Holland.

An informal photo of Dad with the Grocer Dog crew. Dad is standing top left. In his 9-s Dad could still name every man, where they were from, and what happened to them after the war.

We flew together from Grand Island to Bangor, Maine, where we refueled and got some sleep. Then we flew to Goose Bay, Labrador. We were briefed there and then flew to Reykjavik, Iceland. I remember that flight most distinctly because we lost five crews in the North Atlantic, a rate higher than we would normally lose in combat.

It was a beautiful moonlit night all the way from Labrador to Greenland. I could see Greenland off the left wing. Then we hit bad weather. It was terrible weather from sea level to 20,000 feet. The crews we lost used up fuel trying to climb higher above the weather. I remember MacFarland saying "We were briefed to fly at 10,000 feet and I'm flying at 10,000 feet regardless of this weather."

It was a long night, I'll tell you, but the next morning we broke out into clear skies. We had a hard time figuring out where we were, but Mac and I decided we were south of Iceland, so Mac turned north and we picked up our radio signal. We ran out of gas at the end of the runway and coasted to a stop and had to be towed off the runway.

I slept 14 hours that night!

It's not just the hours of flying, it's the tension too, literally hours and hours of white knuckles. The next leg was to Stornoway on the Isle of Lewis, Scotland, and finally to Nutts Corner, Ireland, where we left "Grocer Dog," the call name for our B-17.

We traveled by surface to our assigned base with the 384th Bombardment Group, 247th Squadron, located at Grafton Underwood, almost exactly 70 nautical miles north of London. We were part of the 41st Combat Wing, 1st Air Division, of the Eighth Army Air Force, The other two groups were in Kimbolton and Molesworth. How English can you get? The first night we walked into our barracks, exhausted and loaded down with our gear, and no one greeted us. I finally spoke up and said, "What about some cots for us?" And a bombardier from Akron said, "Take any of those empty beds; they're not coming back."

Grafton Underwood was a real RAF field. Our ordinary missions were flown at about 27,000 feet. I had 31 missions: 15 to France, 15 to Germany, and one to Poznan, Poland. Our targets were always pinpoint: marshaling yards, ball bearing factories, assembly plants for the Messerschmitt, and then the "no ball" targets along the European coastline. We didn't know what they were but they turned out to be the launching sites for the V-1 "buzz bomb" rockets. On our first leave our crew was in London and we were caught in one of the first V1 attacks! There is some real irony there!

Our second leave was on the Western Shore, almost all the way to Scotland, probably Morcambe or Blackpool. It was a vacation spot. It was there that I learned about English "fish and chips," sold at the stands overlooking the beach. Now that I think about it, this was fast food and it was damned good!

I met a nice girl while on leave, Lucy, and Mac dated her friend, Eileen. They were nice girls, wholesome and pretty, and virtuous, who loved to dance. They invited us to their homes for tea and biscuits, to meet their parents. We gave them all the cigarettes we could. Lucy married Joe Chatterton, an infantryman who served with the British in North Africa, opposing the Germans under Erwin Rommel. She and Joe moved to Canada. Lucy died of cancer, and that year Joe sent out their Christmas letter as usual.

The crew of the Grocer Dog. Dad is crouching, second from the left

We were the 41st Combat Wing: Grafton Underwood, Kimbolton, and Molesworth—three bomber groups that formed a wing. For a mission, squadrons assembled at each of the three bases, then we'd assemble the three groups in the air over the South of England to complete the 41st Combat Wing. Then all the wings were assembled to complete the Air Division, which crossed the Channel into enemy territory, into flack and the Luftwaffe.

We flew a feinting route first to mislead the Germans by flying a false flag, and then a correcting leg to take us to our IP (initial point) close to the target. Then we'd turn to the target and the lead bombardier (group leader) would take over the flight controls remotely from his seat. The pilot had to bide his time from the IP to the target point known as the target run.

For each group, the bombardier in the lead plane was the only one active during the target run. When he dropped his bomb the other bombardiers toggled theirs. The bombardier had to arm the bombs as we flew over the English Channel. He would go back to the bomb bay and pull the pins from the detonators. When the pin was in place the bombs couldn't explode. Once he pulled the pins they were armed and no longer safe.

There was a lead navigator for each group. The other navigators followed him, but they also had to maintain the placement of their plane in the wing and keep track of where they were. If your plane was damaged you had to peel off and return to England. You might return to Sweden or Switzerland, neutral territories, if your plane was too damaged to return to England. A B-17 could fly with just two engines, but couldn't hold its altitude with just two engines.

I had high respect for those pilots. That plane was tough, and a good pilot could fly one with an incredible amount of damage. I don't know what their testing was like in training, but they were just 18 and 19 years old like most of the rest of us, yet they were in charge of a four-engine airplane with a lot of responsibility to handle.

I remember one time when we were probably over the Channel or possibly France, where we were reasonably safe. I made my way up to the cockpit and both Mac and Bernie were drenched in perspiration, keeping the plane tucked in as close to the neighboring B-17 as possible. We were a compact group with extensive fire power, and just maintaining that tight formation to protect your plane and your crew, required total concentration. You may have been in the air for only six of eight hours, but the focus and attention required was exhausting.

A B-17 G had twelve 50 caliber machine guns on it. There were usually twelve B-17s in a group making 144 machine guns. That's a lot of fire power designed to drive off the Focke-Wulf Fw 190 and the Messerschmitt Bf 109. They usually attacked from 12 o'clock high and would sweep as one squadron through a group of B-17s, launching their rockets and quickly gaining altitude to avoid our fire power.

The B-17 really could not hold its own against the German fighter planes, and at the beginning, the Eighth Army was losing crews faster than they could be trained.

I found out later, reading a book by one of the German Luftwaffe officers, that at the beginning the Eighth Air Force was used as a decoy on its raids to Berlin. The crews were being sacrificed to draw out the Luftwaffe for the Mustang P51s to attack. Until the arrival of the Mustang in 1944, the Air Force was not holding its own. The only escort plane they had was the Republic P47 Thunderbolt. It could only go two-thirds of the way into France, and then the bombers were unescorted the rest of the way to their target in Germany. The Mustang P51 with its belly tank could go to Berlin and back and even put in 20 minutes of fighting over Berlin.

The earlier Berlin flights were really a sacrifice of the Eighth Air Force crews to soften up the Luftwaffe for D-Day. Fortunately for me and my crew, we got to England in April 1944, just as the P51 was appearing. However, my first flights were with only P47s as escort. Our crew arrived in England after the terrible raids on ball bearing plants at Stuttgart and Regensburg. There is a book on the subject called *Black Thursday.* We were losing, but none of the commanders would admit it. When I got there the commander was Ira Eakear, and he had been preceded by Jimmy Doolittle. Our Colonel was Dale Smith, a West Point graduate.

When I completed my combat tour of 31 missions, I was offered a captaincy and the position of lead navigator. I had no difficulty turning that offer down. The facts were plain: I was alive as a lieutenant and had no wish to come home as a dead captain.

The reason for the 31 missions was that they had set the tour at 30 missions, but no one was making it to 30. So, they changed it to 25. Then, as we gained superiority in the air, they raised it to 30 again, and then to 35. I have credit for 35 missions, but I flew only 31. *[Most of Dad's missions were flown in May and June of 1944.]*

If you completed your tour you automatically got a Distinguished Flying Cross, which I hold. An Air Medal was awarded after five missions, and an oak leaf cluster for every five or ten after that. I flew on D-Day; we bombed Caen at the beaches known as Sword and Juno.

We flew missions on June second, third and fourth. On the fifth, the weather was bad and there were no flights. On June the sixth, I was awakened very early—hours earlier than usual, and told the invasion of France would start that morning. The orderly who woke us up was very excited: "Lieutenant Kinzer, get up! We are invading Europe today!"

Typically, the officers were awakened at 4 on the morning of a mission. We were given a big breakfast, then we all met in the War Room of the barracks to be briefed on our assignments for the day. A large map of Europe was front and center in the room, but covered. When the Duty Officer was sure we were al present and accounted for he removed the covering and revealed our destination. If it was Berlin, a loud collective groan went up. Berline was one of our longest missions and the route was defended the whole way and the whole way back too. Any mission that involved Berlin was a dangerous mission. There would be casualties, the only question was how many.

On June 6th, D-Day. we were divided into three missions. The first group left early and bombed sites that we now know where the locations where the V1 Rocket attacks were launched. We were part of the second mission - bombing bridges and roads outside Caen and the D-Day invasion beaches. After the briefing there was time for more coffee and a smoke. Then the whole crew assembled to check their plane, and then we were off, part of a huge formation, a wing. We were assigned to bomb two specific bridges outside Caen. A third group was assigned to bomb roads that might be used by Germans in response to the invasion. These were long flights - you didn't fly straight for Caen. We feinted towards Pas de Callais, as a diversion, and then corrected to Caen. The flights were carefully orchestrated and I was a busy navigator.

For a long time I thought I had flown two missions on D-Day; that would have been a rarity! But no, I flew two missions—long ones—in 24 hours, which is different.

On June 7th we were sent, before daylight, to cut off German supply-lines and bomb transportation hubs all around Caen. The Allies had seized the initiative and surprised the Germans, but they needed to hold that edge. On June 8th we bombed marshalling yards near Orleans, again, a tactical mission to deny the Germans their supply lines On June 10th we bombed a German airfield near Nantes. June 13th we bombed a German airfield in Dreaux. By early August 1944, I had completed my combat missions with the 38th Bomb Group, but I was still in the Army Air Force. I spent the last of my WWII career delivering B-24 bombers, Liberators, from the US, where they were manufactured in Oklahoma and Texas, to airfields just short of the India Burma Hump.

I was now part of the Air Transport Command and it was boring stuff. Long days of flying. But no one was shooting at you. We'd land in Calcutta and leave the B-24 there. Someone else took it over the Himalaya Hump—that passage required special expertise.

[Dad told me this assignment was much safer, but it meant many long days in the air, flying in loose formation across America to a base in Florida, and then either across to Morocco or down to Brazil, and then across to Africa and on to India. Because of this part of his service Dad flew in all three theaters of War in WWII: Europe, Africa and Asia.]

We'd get a flight back to Delhi, Bombay, or Marrakesh right away. But then we waited until the Command accumulated a planeload of pilots, copilots, and navigators, and they'd fly everyone back to Texas or Oklahoma. Then we'd start it all over again.

I hated Bombay; it was filthy, smelly and the people living there looked pretty wretched, the beggars, the naked children… Marrakesh was more to my liking, exotic, yes, but much cleaner.

By early August 1944, I had completed my combat missions with the 38th Bomb Group, but I was still in the Army Air Force. I spent the last of my WWII career delivering B-24 bombers, Liberators, from the US, where they were manufactured in Oklahoma and Texas, to airfields just short of the India Burma Hump.

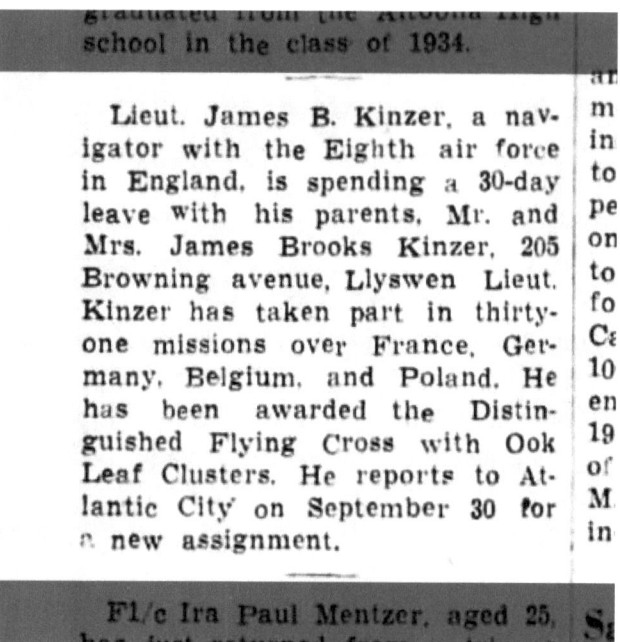

school in the class of 1934.

Lieut. James B. Kinzer, a navigator with the Eighth air force in England, is spending a 30-day leave with his parents, Mr. and Mrs. James Brooks Kinzer, 205 Browning avenue, Llyswen Lieut. Kinzer has taken part in thirty-one missions over France, Germany, Belgium, and Poland. He has been awarded the Distinguished Flying Cross with Ook Leaf Clusters. He reports to Atlantic City on September 30 for a new assignment.

Fl/c Ira Paul Mentzer, aged 25,

The Altoona Tribune, September 12, 1944.

I was now part of the Air Transport Command and it was boring stuff. Long days of flying. But no one was shooting at you. We'd land in Calcutta and leave the B-24 there. Someone else took it over the Himalaya Hump—that passage required special expertise.

I despised Bombay; it was filthy, smelly and the people living there looked pretty wretched, the beggars, the naked children... Marrakesh was more to my liking, exotic, yes, but much cleaner.

I hated barracks life. Period. The smell of so many men in close quarters was highly offensive. The language, the boasting, and the crude behavior were things I wasn't used to and never grew used to. Men are vulgar in large groups. The gambling that took place was appalling and not good for morale. Some men remember the war fondly; they liked the adventure and danger. I was okay with that, but the vulgarity and crudity—I was glad to put that behind me.

One thing I did like about service was getting to see so much of America and meeting and working alongside men from all over the United States. I met men who were better educated than I was and it made me want an education like they had. I met men from big cities who were far more polished and sophisticated than me. But I also met men who had never owned a toothbrush! We had Catholics and Jews at home in Altoona, but we didn't mix much, except at school. The Air Force provided all kinds of life lessons that have served me well.

When you're young, 19 or 20 years old, you have little idea of what could happen to you. We weren't heroes; we did what any other young man did. There is such a thing as male bonding, and we did hang together. Men are like that, not expressing fear or cowardice in front of their peers. Men also recognize a good leader and they will defer to him. I wanted to acquit myself well and fulfill my obligations. I didn't want to lose face, but I didn't need to be a hero, either.

Pete Ziegler was sometimes afraid, I could see fear in his eyes. There was also a guy in our barracks who was headed for a Section 8. A 20 mm shell had exploded in the nose of his B-17, blowing his Bombardier to pieces, and that navigator had had enough. He was on his way home. He just paced back and forth for hours with a silly grin on his face.

Our war in the air was an odd one. We were given a scrumptious breakfast at about 4:00 a.m., were in the air about 6:00 a.m., and then we had a rough time of it for six or eight hours. But when we were back home in the early afternoon, there were steaks and beer for dinner and you could take a nice hot shower every day, twice a day!

It would have felt very different if I was a foot soldier or in the Navy. The Army Air Force was considered a glamorous assignment. At the same time, the Eighth Air Force suffered higher casualties than did the Marines fighting in the South Pacific. The whole experience of war is very strange - but it begins to feel normal pretty quickly, so immersed are you.

Toward the end of my service I had a very odd experience, the kind of experience wartime hands you. As a clean-cut American officer, who happened to be in Florida, I was "requisitioned" to have tea with Fulgencio Batistsa! He was the former president of Cuba, a strong man and close to being a dictator. He had been relocated to Florida in 1944, where he was a "guest" of the United States, or the CIA, perhaps? I joined other officers and we had tea with Batista, he was staying - or held - at a beautiful Florida estate. We were instructed to be sociable and polite, and in the Army you do what you're told. So we ate sandwiches, drank tea, and had a nice time making small talk.

Even so, it was pretty clear the man was an important prisoner. Batista? He was gracious and voluble, a dictator biding his time; he talked about himself at great length.

I feel as though Dad's service in WWII needs some explanation. We are used to the story with a time line that goes: "I registered with my draft board and enlisted all on my 18th birthday! Lots of young men went straight from high school graduation and off to war." That was not the case for Dad. He graduated high school in the winter, a semester early, and went straight to Penn State. He wasn't yet 18.

Jim explained that Dad told him he had seen a photo spread about the Army Air Force in Life or Look magazine, and decided he wanted to be a "fly boy."

Uncle Shorty Williams told Brooks and Jimmy that if Jimmy wanted to be an officer and fly planes he needed to cram in as much college math as he could, and right away. Uncle George's thoughts were of high value: he had seen three of his younger brothers enlist in WWI. He had a better understanding of what was involved and what was at stake and why a little preparation would be good.

Dad registered for the draft at 18 as required, but then he waited to be called up. In the meantime he went to college, since that would be the best way to become an officer. That's why Dad - and his friend Russ - hurried off to Penn State. Their service in the war was inevitable - but how to make the best of it?

When he registered for the draft he designated the Army Air Force on his form. That choice set off a further delay, as space for testing and training had to be found and scheduled. He ended up getting a good three semesters of college before reporting for duty.

# COLLEGE, LAW SCHOOL, MARRIAGE

I returned to college a different Jim Kinzer, with a swelled head, an indifferent attitude, and too much over celebrating on the weekend.

My grade average tumbled. My opinion of myself was overblown. In spite of those and other sins I managed to get by, had many friends, and set my sights high for the future. Chemical engineering was a tough curriculum. Many applied and few were chosen. I was good, even excellent in math and science, which carried me through my courses. Many chums failed due to physical chemistry, but it was apple pie for me.

However, I knew I wouldn't be a good engineer. I'd heard about patents and law, so I went to George Washington Law School with Clyde Metzger, a fraternity brother who was equally motivated. I had real difficulty studying law, but Clyde did well and our friendship helped me.

As you know, I met your Mother [Vaida Belle Riggs, "Snippy," 1927-2003] at Penn State. She was a dimpled darling.

**Snippy's high school graduation picture.**

She was dating a fraternity brother, Fred Nichols, who would be out of town for a big campus dance. He asked me to take his date to the dance and keep the other guys away from her. I agreed, but it all seemed silly to me.

School dances? I'd been to war! That's how I felt about a lot of college life when I returned to campus. This was kid's stuff! And here we Veterans were, plopped down with a bunch of kids. By the calendar we were only a year or two older than our fellow students, but we were men seasoned by war, while they were still kids doing kid stuff.

But as a favor to Fred, I agreed to take his girl to the big dance and keep the other guys away from her. I can still remember the first time I saw her. Well, since Fred was worried about leaving her alone, I figured she was a pretty girl. However, when I picked her up I was still surprised by how pretty she was. I waited in the entrance of her sorority and Snip was looking in a mirror, fixing her hair or adjusting a hat, something like that. She had nice legs. I took a good look at her figure while she was turned away. Then our eyes met in the mirror.

She must have liked what she saw, too. She smiled at me and when I saw her dimples I thought: *My goodness, what a good looking girl! I must get those dimples! I'm going to marry her!*

Yes, I stole my fraternity brothers' girl.

I left Penn State for law school a year before Vaida graduated. I hitchhiked back and forth on weekends when I could, a pretty common way of getting around back then. I had a suitcase with a Penn State sticker, and when I left George Washington I displayed that side of the suitcase for motorists to see. On the return trip I displayed the other side with a GWU sticker on it. When Snippy was home for visits I did the same, hitchhiking to Uniontown to see her.

However there was a good bus service between Uniontown and DC, so I often rode the bus. You could sleep on a bus. Your mother's older half-sister, Cheerful, was dating a man named Emmett. I can't remember his last name but I always liked him, and often he gave me a ride as far as Cumberland on Old Route 40. That route is still a fun drive, slow and scenic.

In Washington DC I bought your mother an engagement ring. I never told Snippy this story. I didn't buy it at a jewelry store: I bought it from a young fellow on campus who had the ring handed back to him. A half-carat diamond in a swell platinum setting! He was lucky to get it back. It was more than I could afford, but he was just glad to be rid of it and I got it at a bargain price.

Snippy was thrilled when she saw the ring I had for her. She was feeling down about spending her senior year alone at the sorority house while everyone else was out partying and dating. So, a really good engagement ring to wear on her finger was important!

To be honest, I didn't have much to give her. Really, just a promise of a better life for both of us. Being engaged to a girl like Snippy gave me a reason to do as well as I could at law school and the Patent Court. I applied myself in a way I never did at Penn State.

I went to law school on the GI bill, in my opinion the best thing the Government ever did for the GIs, but you had to be smart enough to know it was your main chance. I also had a little income as a teaching aid for the chemistry department at GWU. As part of the law school program, I attended law school at night and worked at the Patent Office during the day. This rigor never affected me at the time, and many of us young men worked that way for years without complaint. As you age though, you wonder how you ever worked that way for so long.

After we married, we had a one-bedroom apartment at 2121 H Street. I'm sure that building is long gone: absorbed into the George Washington University campus. We had few possessions and even less money.

I met a lot of great people at the Patent Office and established friendships that have lasted throughout my career. My smart-ass days were finished, principally because I had difficulty in law school. I was genuinely humbled and ready to be a hard worker again.

# CHICAGO, EVANSTON, WILMETTE, AND BACK TO EVANSTON.

We left Washington at the end of February 1951 and moved to the Chicago area. We drove a green Chrysler coupe I bought from my father. We had our first child, Jamie, born June 8, 1950. Everything we owned was packed in the car: crib, ironing board—the lot, and $600 in savings to start our new life.

While working in the Patent Offices I had met Charlie Cannon of the Chicago patent firm Wallace and Cannon. The partners were both older gentlemen. After George Wallace talked to me and made sure I had all my fingers and toes, they brought me into their firm. George Wallace was active with the Medina Temple in Chicago and I'm sure my Masonic association sat well with him.

**"Meet me, but don't walk"** This was Dad's telegram to Snippy, who was staying with her family in Uniontown while Dad went to be interviewed by Cannon and Wallace. He was letting her know he had landed that big job in Chicago,,,and a new adventure was starting.

Our second apartment was in Evanston, a full-floor duplex at 1705 Dempster Street. The duplex is still there. We must have lived on Dempster for a while; Jim was born there in March 1952, and Byron too in August 1953. I recall Jamie trapping her younger brother between the front door and storm door and leaving him there for Snippy to discover.

There was a butcher down the street and when Vaida went there the butcher called her "Missy," which she didn't like, having three children in tow and paying cash. Your mother did not like being taken lightly!

In a short time we bought an empty lot in Wilmette, 2314 Thornwood Avenue near the intersection with Colgate Street. That house was torn down a few years ago and replaced with a much bigger house. I was surprised! That little house was built to last and here it was torn down after 60 years.

I borrowed money from Mother to buy the lot and we purchased plans for a truly modest, single-story home from an architect, a former student of Frank Lloyd Wright.

We were familiar with Frank Lloyd Wright's small homes - Usonian he called them - through one of my patent court judges, Robert Leighey. The Leighey's invited us to their home several times, a very small but beautiful house in Falls Church. This is now known as the Pope-Leighey House.

We had watched a house being built on a vacant lot near our apartment on Dempster. We could see it had some commonality with the Wright house we had been in, so we talked to the people at the worksite, found the architect, and decided we wanted one just like it. It was a modern house, modern-looking, with a flat roof and a carport.

We built that house on a tight budget – there was no mortgage. When I think back on it, I am amazed we took that on! I was a new lawyer, running down every work lead I could. I was up late drafting briefs, and here I was on the weekends digging a foundation and preparing for the slab to be poured, all to save a few dollars!

**Dad with his three oldest in front of the house they built on Thornwood Ave. The home was meant for 5 people, 3 children, so when the twins came along it was only a question of time before we would move again.**

We moved in next door to the Leverenz family. Jack Leverenz paid $3,200 for a corner lot and I paid $3,000 for mine. I borrowed $4,000 from my mother at 4% interest. The house itself wasn't expensive to build and went up quickly. A living room, a dining room, just the one bathroom, a small kitchen with a little eat-in nook, three bedrooms and a carport. On a cement slab.

**The house was small and modest, but it still had some Wrightian flair, like this Roman Brick fireplace with sandstone ledge.**

Modest but special too. It was a nice brick house designed by an architect and of course it included some special touches - a large brick fireplace with a long stone ledge for the hearth, a big picture window, a small but very modern kitchen with a breakfast nook. It was all that anyone wanted or expected in 1954.

The backyard was big, with plenty of room for playing. In no time we had a swing set and a sandbox, then a tree fort, a little patio right by the kitchen door for the picnic table and grill, and a nice fence to keep you kids in. Snippy had a little vegetable garden - rhubarb, peppers and tomatoes. Harper School and a sports field were just down the street.

We were both proud of that house.

When the twins were born, the Thornwood house was too small for all seven of us. We had the carport closed in and it became a fourth bedroom, but there was still only the one bathroom, and we knew we would have to move again in the next few years. We got a TV then, after the twins were born, your Mom needed it to get you kids out of her hair long enough to get dinner cooked and on the table.

And that reminds me, it was oh, late May of 1956 and Snippy was pregnant. We were hoping for a baby sister so Jamie could have some company. But there was Vaida, and she was huge. I said to her: I think you are having twins! She laughed at me and I said: I mean it. You've been big, but you've never been *this* big! She burst into tears because she knew I was right. Twins, that was a lot to contemplate.

She called her doctor and went to see him the next day. He could only hear one heart beat but he agreed Vaida looked like she was full term, but she wasn't due until mid July.

There's only one heart beat, the doctor said, but sometimes when twins are close together the hearts align and they develop a sympathetic heartbeat in the womb. He took an x-ray, it cost $25!, and there they were: twins! They were born two weeks later, six weeks early, 4 and 5 pounds. They kept Snippy in the hospital for a full week, to rest. Mother came out by train to help me. But the twins were kept in incubators. Janet came home after a week, and then Margaret came home after another week.

But this delay in the appearance of the twins caused some embarrassment for Jamie, Jimzy and Barney. They told all their friends they were having twins and now there were no babies at all! They got called out for fibbing by all their little buddies. Meme was considered a more reliable witness and she assured the children of Thornwood Ave and Harper School that the twins really did exist.

I insisted the doctor give me the x-ray, I'd paid for it after all. Really I just wanted it - because it was pretty amazing to see.

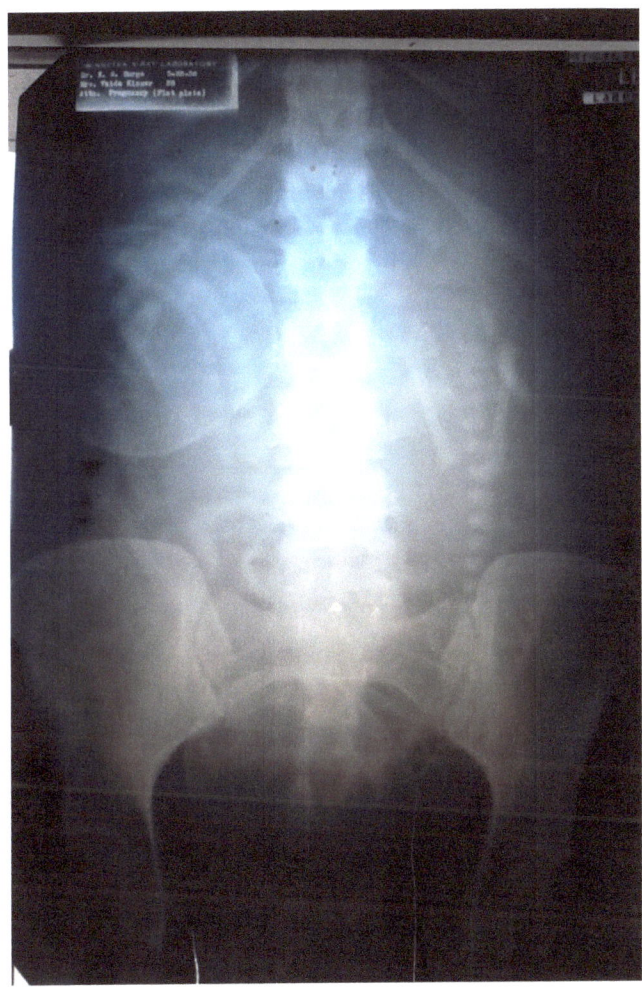

**The Famous $25 X-ray that Dad insisted on keeping.**

The men in the neighboring families were mostly veterans starting out their careers. Most of them were college graduates, both the husbands and the wives. The men were all working to regain the years they'd lost to military service. We were all in a hurry to start over and get on with life.

I recall frequently bringing work home. Snippy and I would get you kids bathed and tucked in. Then she'd settle in with the evening paper or the New Yorker and I'd get out my legal work, spread it out on the dining room table, and work late into the night.

We were all leading a suburban life, everyone around us, centered on our marriages and children. The weekends were spent with your family - chores, church, getting the grill out, kids playing in the street. Not like today with country clubs, careers and travel. This was home life then. Boring? Maybe. But it shows our commitment

During the Red Scare there was an informal committee in our neighborhood. Some people wanted to build and stock a bomb shelter - to survive a Nuclear attack by the Ruskies. I didn't believe we would have a nuclear war, but I understood that fear. However, building a bomb shelter was sheer nonsense, a bandaid. I argued against it, heated words were exchanged, and there were hard feelings in the neighborhood. It was a crazy idea to think that our little neighborhood in Wilmette could ride-out a nuclear attack in a shared cement bunker.

Nuclear war, the Red Scare and the Rosenbergs. Three things that were a dividing line in the Eisenhower era. I was more conservative than many of our neighbors, and Vaida was usually a little more conservative than me, but inclined to keep her opinions to herself, more so than me. We were often out-of-step with our peers.

Snippy and I always saw eye-to-eye on the big things. She was not one to keep up with the Joneses, and neither was I. We had both been to college and we wanted that for you kids. Saving for tuition was always on our minds. We were both readers and independent thinkers, and we wanted to raise readers who were independent thinkers. Snippy wasn't a frivolous spender like so many other wives. I relied on her. I handed my paycheck over to her and she ran the household, including the finances. She took her obligations seriously, and so did I.

We stayed in Wilmette until we moved to Lawndale Avenue in Evanston in the early 1961s. Snippy picked the house on Lawndale and I'm glad she did. The realtor kept showing her these huge old houses, closer to the lake. Brick-a-brack houses, fancy ones on big lots. You could buy them cheap in 1961. But Snippy said that kind of a house required hired help to maintain and she wasn't used to that and didn't want it. She wanted a bigger house, but one she could manage on her own - and that was 2409 Lawndale Ave.

After we signed the mortgage at the bank on Central Street - we felt like we needed a drink. It was the middle of the day but we wanted a drink! Evanston was dry as a bone, but the yonder side of Crawford was Skokie.

We drove to Ed's UBAA for a drink, and that may have been the last time I persuaded your Mother to go there. We had just signed a thirty year mortgage for $33,000 a sum of money we thought we'd never live to see. Remember Thornwood was less than $10,000 - land, foundation, house, furnishings. I financed it with savings and a loan from my Mother. But the house on Lawndale was another matter altogether! We'd had to go to a bank and bare our souls for their scrutiny. So we had a round of drinks and toasted our future as slaves to a mortgage. *This is where his memoirs ended.*

This little photo of Jamie, Jim, and Barney, battered and crumbling, was in Dad's wallet the day he died. Dad was an emotional and feeling man in a generation of men that were discouraged from being sentimental.

# SOME NOTES ABOUT DAD'S FAMILY

His Great-Grandparents: Rev. John Andrew Jackson Williams, Civil War veteran, carpenter, and lay-minister, 1833-1909, and his wife, Mary Jane Gilliland Willams, 1837-1926.

**George W. Mauk,** 1832-1863, a farmer who was injured at Antietam and died in Washington, DC at the Soldiers Home. His wife/widow, **Susan Fry Mauk Myers,** 1836-unknown, remarried to **Sam                                                                              Myers**.

**His Grandparents: James Shane Williams,** 1862-1932, a bookkeeper and civic leader, and his wife **Annetta Mauk Williams,** 1862-1930, a Civil War orphan. They married in 1881, and had 12, children, 8 boys and 4 girls.

**His Parents: James Brooks Kinzer,** 1899-1964. Known as Brooks to his family, and Poppy to his grandchildren. His wife, **Mary Lillian Williams,** 1900-1994. Called Lillian, she was known as Meme to her 13 grandchildren and many great-grandchildren.

**His Siblings**:   **JoAnn Vivian Kinzer Reese,** 1929-2000. JoAnn married Robert Reese, our "Uncle Bob." They lived in Hollidaysburg and are the parents of our cousins: Terri, Robert Jr, Lynn, and Shane. **JohnGary Kinzer,** 1938-2013, known as Gary. Gary married Marjorie Hammond, "Aunt Margie." They lived in Kansas, near Margie's family, and are the parents of our cousins Kelli, Bronwyn, Garin, and Leigh.

**His Wife and children: Vaida Belle Riggs Kinzer**, "Snippy," December 24, 1927 - May 22, 2003. Snippy had grown up in a big family and she was the classic middle child - but far from a push-over, as the family nick-name conveys. Snippy she was called, and Snippy she was!

She told me that Meme's marital advice to her, on her wedding day no less, was never to contradict or correct Jimmy in front of another person - hold your tongue, wait and do it in private! "I always followed that rule with Brooks," Meme said to her, "and it makes for a happy marriage. Let him be the King of his Home in public and keep your disagreements private." Mom always repeated this story with a little laugh.

Ann Jamison Kinzer, June 8, 1950, James Brooks Kinzer, March 27, 1952 - Dec 16, 2024, John Byron Kinzer, August 22, 1953, Margaret Kirk Kinzer Meyers and Janet Deering Kinzer, June 15, 1956.

**1959 - James Jr., Janet, Margaret, John Byron, and Ann Jamison**

**Meme's Brothers and Sisters:** These are Meme's siblings; most of them Dad knew well because he grew up among them in Roaring Spring. The boys were all named for Methodist bishops the family knew.

**John Merrill,** 1881-1954. The oldest, called "Merril." He was the minister who married Mom and Dad in 1949. As Dad put it: "Well, he married everyone and buried them too." His wife was Carrie; they had no children. Merrill was well-educated and held many important posts in the Methodist hierarchy, and he had several good appointments." He died of chronic myocarditis.

**George Bowman,** 1883-1947. George was one of Dad's favorite uncles and an important mentor. He was the head of the math department at Altoona High School. He was known as "Shorty Williams." and for good reasons: according to his WW1 draft card, he was 5 '4" and about 130 pounds. He was married to Lucretia for 40 years, but they had no children, which perhaps explains his attachment to Dad. George was unusually well-educated - with degrees from Dickinson and Penn State. He continued his post-graduate work through-out his 40 year career as a teacher at Altoona HS, where he was also the head of the Department. He had to retire early due to chronic asthma, which killed him soon after retiring.

**Bessie Celestia,** 1885-1902. She died at age 17 and is buried with her parents. A classmate, as a prank, nicked her with a pocket knife and she died of blood poisoning. There were no antibiotics and she died slowly, at home, with the whole family witnessing it. The family endured three such tragedies: Bessie, Ruth and Paul.

**Ruth Susan,** 1886-1900, or maybe Susan Ruth, but known as Ruth. Ruth died at age 14 of a concussion: she was leaning back in a chair when the chair legs slipped. She hit the back of head and fell into a coma. This story was repeated to us whenever Meme saw us leaning our chair backwards.

**James Ross,** 1888-1919. Known as Ross, he's a bit of a mystery. The family said he was a drinker and that he was sent away due to shame over his alcoholism. This is what Meme also told Dad about her brother. Otherwise not much was said about him in the family, but he was brought home to die and an obituary appeared in the paper.

Dad mentions that Ross Williams was sent to Arizona to "dry out," but Dad further speculates that Ross was syphilitic as well.

According to his obituary, James Ross Williams was 31 when he died and had been living away from home for 7 years, indicating that he left the area around 1912 when he would have been 24 or so. In the 1910 census he is living with his parents, 22, and no occupation. When he registered for the draft in June of 1917 he was listed as being a waiter at the Davenport Hotel, an historic hotel still in operation. On his WW1 draft form Ross is described as being medium height, with a slight build and no apparent disabilities. (We can see he is slight from the two photos we have of him.)

When the family got news that he was dying, in March of 1919, he was brought home by train to spend his last months with his family and he died in October 1919, with his family present. So, perhaps the Williams family wasn't as harsh as Dad makes them sound. His death certificate doesn't list syphilis; it says he was an invalid and died of chronic valvular heart disease lasting 19 years. So, the doctor dated the condition, an outcome of long-term syphilis, back to when Ross was 12(!) Perhaps the doctor was being kind to the Williams family by listing the true, immediate, cause of death, while obscuring the origins.

**Clara Vivian**, 1893-1952. She became Mrs. Frank McDermott and moved to Akron, Ohio as a young woman. The family never had much contact with Clara, who was sickly once she moved to Akron.

**Edwin Witman,** 1894-1951. As a young man Ed moved to Altoona and then Pittsburgh, where he was an engineer for a gas company. He died at a veteran's hospital of "cerebral softening" caused by a hemorrhage. (Death certificate) When Dad knew his Ed he was married to Alfaretta, a young widow with a son. They had two boys who died young, and one daughter who died of diphtheria at age one.

Dad recalls Uncle Ed as a drinker, and a tragic figure, under-employed with an easy but low-paying job, and like Ross, another family outcast.

But he was much more than that. Edwin was a combat veteran of WWI. He was a corporal in the 110th Infantry, 28th Division, an all

Pennsylvania division, called the "Iron Division" and the "Men of Iron" because of their hand-to-hand combat with Germans at the Battle of Chateau-Thierry. He enlisted in June of 1916 and was discharged in May of 1919. He served in the front lines for about 7 months.

Before the war he graduated from Dickinson in Williamsport, where many of his family went to college. After the war he went to Penn State and then Bucknell, where he graduated in 1924 with a degree in Chemical engineering. He's a handsome man in his yearbook photo: "Ed made his first appearance in Lewisberg in September 1922. It was evident that this was inevitable since *Mrs Ed* is a former Bucknellian. If you want Ed in a hurry, look for him at Howard Stahl's place of business and you'll probably hear him exclaim "Three ball, cross corner, watch it go!"

Suddenly, Ed sounds like fun!

But who is the "Mrs Ed" mentioned in the year book entry? It seems Mrs Ed is Fay M. Schoch, born in Huntingdon in 1896. The Altoona newspaper announced their war-time marriage in 1918, and yes, she is a 1917 graduate of Bucknell where she was trained to be a teacher. Rev J. Marrill Williams presided. I don't find a marriage certificate, I don't find a divorce.

The only other evidence of their marriage is two death certificates. One is for an infant son who died in 1923, one day after his birth. The next is for their son, Edwin W Williams Jr, who died in 1935 aged not quite 15 - of "Malnutrition due to lack of development. 15 years duration." (Death certificate) He was living in Huntingdon with his mother and her parents. She is using her maiden name. In the 1930 Census Fay and her son "Billy," the older Schoch's own a jewelry store where Fay works.

And now I am wondering if Dad has confused things. Perhaps Edwin was the brother with syphilis, rather than Ross. Afterall, Ed served in France and may have picked up the disease while in the military, he wouldn't be the first. His one son has some congenital condition that handicaps him to the point that he dies of malnutrition, and the second child dies one day after birth. It could be bad luck, or it could be the natural outcome of syphilis.

The next bit of news comes in 1925 when Miss Minna Lee McClelland, announces her engagement to Edwin W. Williams in the newspaper, but Miss Minna Lee remains Miss Minna Lee for another 20 years, the engagement is broken. We can surmise that sometime after the birth of the second baby in 1923 and the announcement of an engagement in 1925 Ed and Fay were divorced.

But there's another layer to this genealogical onion. Dad mentions Alfaretta, Ed's wife. On Feb 22, 1930, the St Louis Star and Times newspaper in Missouri, lists Edwin W. Williams and Alfretta Saylor Keagy of Altoona, PA, among the couples taking out a marriage license in that city. Are they a run-away couple, or two people finally making it legal? We don't know. In my estimation, Edwin is among the most interesting members of this generation.

**Paul Foster,** 1896-1917. He was employed as a machinist in Altoona, working for the Pennsylvania Railroad. He had enlisted to fight in WWI, like two of his older brothers, but he died before reporting to training camp, one day after a one-car accident when he hit a large oak tree. Paul was a lively and fun-loving young man, and sorely missed by his family. That part we knew from Meme's talking about her family.

The car accident was bad enough to make it into the local newspapers. That reporting tells us that Paul was the last of three young men to die from a late night "joy ride" that ended in a smash-up just outside Hollidaysburg. All three boys had enlisted for service in WWI and were getting ready to report for duty. The two others were killed on impact, but Paul was thrown from the car. He suffered extensive internal injuries and died a painful death 36 hours later. The Altoona Times noted: "The families of the deceased young men, all of whom are the best people in Roaring Spring, have the sincere sympathy of their friends in their great bereavement."

We can see here that the Williams family endured some great losses: Ruth dying of a concussion in 1900, Bessie lost to blood poisoning in 1902, Paul's death in 1917, and then Ross's death in 1919. You can add to that: Byron and Ed going off to war in Europe, and then Byron returning an invalid.

**Byron Joyce,** 1898-1982. He was a veteran of WWI, married to Alice. His wedding announcement from December 26, 1933, says he was badly injured at Argonne and was part of the Rainbow Division (42nd Infantry Division), made up of men from the National Guard in 26 states.

As Dad mentions, Byron was hospitalized several times, to reopen his chest wound and remove blood clots. In his 30s his health improved, treatments improved, and he married Alice and they started a family together. When he registered for the draft in WW11 he was 6 feet tall and 160 pounds. The Williams family came in two sizes: very short and very tall. The "serious gunshot wound to chest" was noted in his death certificate. Even so he lived to be 84, perhaps due to his very happy marriage to Aunt Alice.

**Mary Lillian,** 1900-1994, Meme, Dad's mom. Meme had been to teacher's college before her marriage. "I think she was the family darling, along with baby brother Carl. There weren't many girls in the family, two sisters having died young, so naturally the girls were considered special." Meme was a loving and generous woman. She was very motherly, warm and playful.

In our photos you can see that Meme resembles her Mother, Nettie. They were very close, which is easy to understand since Nettie lost two of her daughters - Bessie and Ruth - while Mary Lillian wasstill a baby.

**Glenn Vincent,** 1902-1977. Glenn was a pharmacist at Williams Pharmacy in Roaring Spring. Sometime after his marriage, they moved to Philadelphia where he owned a large pharmacy, with the family living above the store. Even when he lived far away he was a regular visitor to Roaring Spring and attended all the family weddings and funerals. Glenn and Sally Ann were social and fun-loving people. Dad was sweet on Glenn's daughter, Sally Ann.

After a happy time in Philadelphia, Glenn's family returned to Roaring Spring - a theme for this generation of children: Ross is brought home to die, Glenn returns to run a store, Meme returns to care for her parents, Merrill returns towards the end of his career to minister at the family church

**Carl Hurlburt,** 1904-1986,"Uncle Hon," as in "Honey," As the youngest he was everyone's pet and it was said that Hon never walked two steps until he got too big for anyone to carry him.

Carl was married to Hazel Kemberlin, an attractive and enterprising woman who proved her mettle many times over.Hazel's family experienced hardship, and she was well-acquainted with the arts of "making do." Because he was the youngest, the Great Depression, with its loss of employment opportunities, probably hit him the hardest of the whole family. Carl drove delivery trucks and worked as a postal clerk.

Carl and Hazel remained in Roaring Spring all his life, as did Meme. Meme was very sad when Carl died, he was her last sibling. She survived him by eight years. His passing "tore at her heart," she said, so they had a strong bond.

Dad's great-grandparents:William Alexander Kinzer, 1823-1864, a subsistence farmer, and his wife Mary Ann Murphy Kinzer, 1826-1904.

**James F. Kirk,** 1831-1900, store owner and farmer, and hiswife **Hannah Dearing Kirk**, 1836-1884

Dad's grandparents:William "Will" Alexander Kinzer, 1863-1932, a subsistence farmer, and his wife Margaret, "Maggie" Lauver Kirk Kinzer, 1872-1950

**Dad's kinzer aunts and uncles: Catherine Mary Kinzer,** 1901-1994, married to Lehman Newton Kirk. They had three children and remained in the Tuscarora/Reeds Gap area where Lehman kept a store.

**Byron Rosell Kinzer**, 1909-1969, "Uncle Bairn" as Dad pronounced his name, also spent his lifetime in the immediate area of Reeds Gap and Honey Grove. He married Anna Earnest in 1935. In the 1940 and 1950 census he is listed as working for the State. He was a game warden. They had one son, Craig, born in 1940.

**William Cecil Bivon Kinzer**, 1914-1969. In the 1940 Census, when he was 25, he was listed as a typist, with two years of college, living with his mother. He married Lois Walker in 1942, and by then he is a teacher. In 1951 his family moved to Milan, Tennessee where he worked for Harvey Aluminum. He died of a heart attack in 1969. They had no children and Lois died only a few months after Bivon.

**Brooks Kinzer, with his mother Maggie, Spring, 1950. This photo was fro Brooks' last visit with his Mother, she died in May that year. Maggie was an important influence on her son and grandson.**

From his memoirs, it is clear that Brook's family was important to Dad while he was growing up. He loved his summer visits to the farm and he learned a lot of life's lessons there. Reeds Gap has great meaning to Dad... but then life intervened: the farm was sold, and then there was the war and then college. As an adult Dad did not pursue contact with Bivon, who had moved away from Pennsylvania. And he only saw his Uncle Byron as part of the occasional visits to his parents. Bivon's death in Tennessee in 1969, like Maggie's missed funeral in 1950, "burdened my conscience" as Dad said to me.

This was a source of some distress for Dad as he aged. He thought his neglect was embarrassing and showed him to be both ungrateful and fickle. These thoughts plaqued him when he was down. He had been an ungrateful child and an ungrateful man he would say. I told him I didn't see it that way. If you look at the 20 years following Dad's military service he was incredibly busy: finishing college, going to law school, marriage, moving to Chicago, starting a career, building his law firm, providing for five children and being hands-on father. All of that in 20 years. I think his family was proud of him and understood why he was not phoning or writing.

But yes, there probably was an element of Dad having "outgrown" those parts of his family. A common fault.

## Early Veterans in the Kinzer and Riggs Family Tree

Using Ancestry.com I found service records, muster rolls, pensions awarded to widows and DAR applications for these men who were direct line ancestors of Jim and Vaida. Parts of Mom's family (Riggs and Stollar) have been in America since the 1650s, so naturally her line provides us with the most veterans in the Revolutionary War.

### *The Revolutionary War*

**David Gilliland, 1744-1784.** A lieutenant in the Middlesex County, New Jersey Militia. (Kinzer side of the family) He served in what was then the "frontier" in Pennyslvania. **Matthew Brown, 1732-1777.** Died of camp fever or typhoid fever, usually from contaminated food or water, while serving in the Flying Camp of 10,000 militia volunteers recruited in Pennsylvania, Maryland, and Delaware. This was a strategic reserve of soldiers requested by Washington, formed in 1776. (Kinzer side of the family)

**Joseph Riggs, 1740-1829.** From Middlesex County, New Jersey. (Riggs side of the family)

**Obadiah Higbee, 1732-1808.** He served in the Second Regiment of the Middlesex County Militia during the Revolution. (Riggs side of the family)

**Rev. David Phillips, 1742-1829.** Phillips was born in Wales but marries here in America in 1763. He was an early organizer serving in the Revolutionary War, along with three brothers, He was a captain in the Second Company, 7th Battalion, Pennsylvania Militia, Chester County, Pennsylvania (Riggs side of the family)

**Robert Bell, 1753-1837.** A private serving as an assistant to the New Jersey Commissary of Services, in Morristown and Hackensack, through the war into 1780. (Riggs side of the family)

**John Michael Paulus Mate, (Matthieu) 1729-1789.** Born in Germany, mustered April 3, 1778, as a Private in a regiment of the Continental Army "on foot." Please note that the man is coming up on 50 years old when he becomes a foot soldier. (Riggs side of the family)

**Andrew McKee, 1747-1833.** Born in Londonderry, Ireland, he enlisted as a Private in March 1776, serving 16 months. He re-enlisted in June 1780. (Riggs side of the family)

**John Machan, 1750-1832.** A Corporal in the Fifth Battalion (Cumberland County Militia) from December 1776 through March 1780. (Riggs side of the family)

**John M. Rockefeller, 1742-1832,** a lieutenant in Hunterdon County Militia, New Jersey, serving from April 1775 through the end of the war, including the Battle of Monmouth. June 28, 1778. (Riggs side of the family)

**Peter Aller, 1742-1817.** His name appears on a muster roll/pay for a New Jersey regiment, Crane's Troops of Horse, 1780. (Riggs side of the family)

**Reuel Sayre,1754-1841.** A lieutenant in the Cumberland County New Jersey Militia, he was at the Battle of Quinton's Ridge, March 18, 1778. According to an account of the Battle, Sayre was surprised by the British, the only member of the night watch to escape capture. (Riggs side of the family)

**Timothy Hunt, 1734-1814.** A Private in the Tryon County Militia, Third Regiment, New York (Riggs side of the family)

## *The War of 1812*

Rev Thomas Rowland Williams, 1776-1858. A Welsh
immigrant and boatman by trade, he fought in the War of
1812, enlisting late in the war. "!776" is probably an
adopted birth date, but he would have been in his 40s
when he joined up to fight in Kentucky.

**Frederick Deering, (Diering or Dearing) 1786-1866.** He
enlisted in 1814 and served for eight months in the Virginia Militia. In
1866, Congress created pensions for veterans of the War of 1812, and
Deering applied for a pension, awarded to him shortly before he died.
He signed the paperwork with an X. (Kinzer side of the family)

### *The Civil War*

Only New York drafted soldiers in the Civil War; those listed
here volunteered for service.

**George W. Mauk, 1832-1863.** A 90-day recruit in the
Pennsylvania 125th Volunteer Infantry, composed of men from Blair,
Huntingdon, and Cambria Counties. In July 1862 he survived the
terrible engagement in the cornfields at Antietam in September,
suffering an injury. He died of typhoid fever at St. Aloysius Hospital
(K and North Capitol Streets, Washington DC. He is buried on the
grounds of the Soldier's Home in Washington DC. His grave still has

the original marker, inscribed "MANK." The cemetery knows the name is misspelled, and offered a new marker, but Dad wanted to leave the original, weathered, stone.

From the NPS website about the Antietam Battlefield: "The 125th Pennsylvania Volunteer Infantry was recruited in Blair, Huntingdon, and Cambria Counties and moved at early dawn from bivouac on the farm of George Line to East Woods near the point where Gen. J.K.F. Mansfield was mortally wounded. From there, the 125th went to support Monroe's First Rhode Island battery on Smoketown Road, then to the woods that stood there on September 17, 1862.

The 125th was the first Union regiment there. Far advanced and without sufficient support, it was outflanked by the enemy and retired behind batteries in the rear field, subsequently saving the guns of Monroe's Battery from capture. The regiment remained in line until the close of battle. Losses at Antietam: Killed and died of wounds 54; seriously wounded 91.(Kinzer side of the family)

**William Alexander Kinzer, 1823-1864.** Served in the Union Army, 173rd Regiment, Pennsylvania Volunteers in 1862 and 1863. In the weeks following Gettysburg, the 173rd chased Lee south and guarded the rail lines in August. He spent about ten months in service. He died in August 1864, a year after being discharged. It isn't clear if he was injured in battle or simply died young. His widow, Mary Ann Murphy Kinzer drew a pension when the war was over. (Kinzer side of the family)

**Rev. John Andrew Jackson Williams, 1833-1909**. The son of Rev. Thomas Rowland William, and named for General Andrew Jackson. In 1864 he was 31, married for ten years and a father, when he joined C Company of the 67th Regiment, Pennsylvania Infantry. We are told that he was a "reluctant volunteer" who felt a true calling as a Minister - not a soldier. Even so, he was in the thick of everything during his service, including a long passage with Sheridan in the Shenandoah Campaign, the siege and fall of Petersburg, and the final pursuit of Lee to Appomatox. Rev. Kinzer was in DC when he was mustered out in July 1865. (Kinzer side of the family)

**The Rev James Andrew Jackson Williams**

## AFTERWORD

When Jim Kinzer and Vaida Riggs married in 1949 they joined two families with long ties to America, all the way back to decades when there were both Dutch and English colonies in the New World.

Vaida's family goes even further back than Dad's. Mom's father, George W. Riggs, is the descendent of Edward Riggs (1589, Roydon England, 1671, Massachusetts Bay Colony), who arrived in the New World in 1633. Pearl Stollar, Vaida's mother, is descended from the Van Der Stollar family and many other Dutch immigrants who settled in the Dutch Colonies of New York when it was still called New Amsterdam. In general, Mom's family arrived in America two generations earlier than Dad's.

For the first few generations of any immigrant family there is a tendency to marry like with like. The Dutch and English parts of Mom's family certainly followed this model for nearly 100 years: the Dutch married Dutch, and the English married English.

Dad's family is a little different. We carry a German sur-name, but those Kinzer men, one after the other, took English and Scots women as their wives, so generation by generation, weKinzers retained our German last name but steadily became more and more English, Welsh, and Scots.

Another thread that joins Mom and Dad's family histories is the search for religious freedom. There are probably many more examples in our family tree, but those are the three examples I have been able to uncover.


• The Van Der Stolars of Kinderdijk, Holland lived in Switzerland for two generations, beginning in the 1560s. Their move coincided with the conclusion of the Eighty Years War, a long complex insurrection that upended Holland and much of Northern Europe. When it was finally settled, Holland had a *Catholic Kingfrom Spain!* In response, the Van der Stolars, reformed protestants, abandoned Holland and settled in Bubendorf near Basel, Switzerland, where they lived for about 50 years. Realizing that not much had changed in Holland, despite having a Catholic King, the family returned to

Kinderdjik, and after a decade of two, some of their sons then immigrated to America.

• The Williams family is part of an early Welsh settlement in America. Around 1795-1797 Ebensburg in western Pennsylvania became the new home of 50 Welsh families. They were Protestant fundamentalists and considered religious dissenters at home. Morgan John Rhys was their leader. He was a radical, and a visionary, who formed the Cambria Company, an enterprise to fund Welsh immigration. Benjamin Rush, his wealthy Quaker benefactor, paid for the settlement in the area that became Cambria County, Pennsylvania—the Latin name for Wales, not the English name.

• The Gilliands: In 1685, our ancestor John Gilliand, of Edinburgh, Scotland, was imprisoned and his goods were confiscated. During his imprisonment he was given a chance to repent - but he refused - and he was shipped off with his family to work a plantation in New Jersey. His ears were cropped - the mark of a heretic! What was his crime? He was a militant Presbyterian, a Covenanter, who refused to denounce his religion. He was lucky to escape with his life.

Finally, both Mom and Dad's families were part of America's earliest westward migration.

As the colonies became more settled, the fourth and fifth generations found that farmland was scarce in the original colonies. The Atlantic coast was fully settled. People began to head west into the frontier of the Shenandoah Valley, where they could then go south into Virginia or north up into the Alleghenies to start new settlements where good farmland was readily available. Our two families headed north and settled in western Pennsylvania when it was still wilderness.

Mom's family probably came by wagon and used the Braddock Road, a military road built in 1755. It was the precursor of the National Highway. We surmise this because Mom's family - the Van der Stollar name was shortened to "Stollar" - settled just a few miles off the old Braddock Road in the area where Washington and Fayette Counties meet in the southwestern corner of Pennsylvania. Dad used to tease Mom because she was the only real hillbilly in the family.

Mom's father was a "Riggs." Edward and Elizabeth Holmes Riggs immigrated to New Jersey in 1633. Landing in Boston when it was still the Massachusetts Bay Colony. They came here from Essex, England, and settled in Essex County, New Jersey. They were there for four generations before heading west.

The Kinzers settled a little further north, perhaps going by riverboat, as Dad speculated. This makes sense, since his family settled in Mifflin and Juniata counties in south central Pennsylvania, an area that is easily reached by river using flatboats.

The Kinzers are Palatinate Germans, protestants from the Rhine Valley, who probably came over in the late 1720s or early 1730s. There was no Germany at that time, just princely states that were still part of the Holy Roman Empire, so they were Protestants living under the grace of Catholic princes. They landed in Philadelphia and made their way to nearby Lancaster County. Later, someone in the Kinzer family migrated further west to Juniata and Mifflin counties.

At the time, those were extremely remote parts of America and the record-keeping was scant. However, both family names appear to be living in Pennsylvania in the first U.S. Census of 1790. We can be proud of that.

Dad mentions the Kinzer families in Lancaster PA, but I can't draw a direct line from one of those families to our family. The line breaks with William Kinzer, 1823-1863. We don't know who his parents were. The first few census lists show the household head by name, and there are Kinzers listed, but then it simply enumerates the other members by gender and age.

In 1794 there was a Pennsylvania tax record for a Jacob Kinzer, owner of a distillery in Greenwood, part of Mifflin County. Three decades later in 1821 there were more Kinzers listed for taxes: Jacob, David and Joel, all distillers. One of these men may be the father of the mysterious William Kinzer.

William was married to Mary Ann Murphy, 1826-1904. Her family, the Murphys, settled in the Honey Grove and Lack area. What I'm trying to say is that while we don't know much about the origins of William Kinzer, I doubt he was a mystery to those living in the region at that time. The Murphys would not have married their daughter to a poor man who was also a stranger, so they must have known him and his family.

When you look at a map you can see all those place names—Greenwood, Port Royal, Mifflintown, Lack, Black Log and Reeds Gap, all located within five, ten, or twenty miles of each other in a long valley created by the Juniata River and confined by the Tuscarora and Shade mountain ranges. Even on foot you could get to the next town in half-day of walking.

Dad's great-grandfather, William Kinzer, was a farmer who died young, just a year after completing military service in the Civil War. Perhaps he returned home injured, we don't know. His wife, Mary Ann Murphy, was a young widow left with several children, including Will, the baby of the family, who would become Dad's grandfather. The Widow Kinzer was lucky in one way: she had the Murphy family all around her. Dad mentions being surrounded by his Murphy cousins.

In 2015 Dad and the twins (Janet and Margaret) went to Greenfield Village in Michigan. One of the many historic homes preserved by Ford was a typical Pennsylvania-Dutch log cabin, consisting of one room with a large fireplace, a sleeping loft accessed by a ladder, and two small windows, both with sturdy wooden hatches that could be braced. The floor was usually dirt covered with straw. During the day the door was open, allowing in more light and air. But at night, with the door closed and the bolt thrown, it was like a tiny fortress in the wilderness.

Dad was moved by this humble display. He said it was very like the ones he saw as a boy, including one that Brooks had pointed out to him as the home that Grandfather Will Kinzer grew up in.

This photo was taken at Greenfield Village, in Michigan. It is a preserved example of typical Pennsylvania log cabin.. Dad was very excited about seeing it and said it was almost exactly like the one pointed out to him by Brooks, as the birthplace of Will Kinzer. Literally a one room home with a sleeping loft and four tiny windows.

The Williams family immigrated from Wales around 1795, we know they were part of the original settlers at Ebensburg in Cambria, PA. That area was settled by Welsh religious nonconformists in the late 1790s. Unfortunately, the Williams family name is very common, but there is a William S. Williams of the right age in the 1800 US Census for Ebensberg.

"Our" William S. Williams (1764-1853) and his wife, Hannah Rowland, along with their son, Rev. Thomas Rowland Williams (1776 - 1858) immigrated together to Ebensberg, Pennsylvania, and all are buried in nearby Beulah.

Dad did not seem to know about this part of the family story - but he would have liked it.

But, as he says he didn't like the Williamses as much as he did the Kinzers. So let's unpack that.

In fairness to the Williamses, I think Dad's poor opinion may have been based on his dislike of his grandfather, James Shane Williams.

In the stories Dad told us, James Shane was always the starchy forbidding patriarch. A brusk, judgmental kind of guy with high standards he imposed on everyone, especially his nearest and dearest.

He seems to have turned out one son, Ed, for drinking, and banished another son, Ross. Keep in mind that for a staunchly Methodist family, any kind of drinking was a sin.

If James Shane was an especially disagreeable old man he had good cause: his wife was dying of kidney failure and he was suffering from prostate cancer. The cherry-on-top of an old man's misery might well have been the Great Depression wiping out his savings and investments.

Even so, as the patriarch of a large family he fully expected his youngest daughter - and son-in-law - to drop everything and move back home to take care of him, which they did. And that could also be the source of Dad's animus: competition for his mother's attention.

Besides taking up all of his mother's time, James Shane would whack you with his cane if he thought you were talking too much or showing off. Dad, a smart and lively little boy, was encouraged by his parents to speak up and stand out. But James Shane Williams had other opinions about that and wanted his grandson to remain silent at the table.

That kind of insult was exactly what a bright and rather willful boy like Jimmy Kinzer, used to being the center of attention, would feel keenly. I really do think that was the root of his dislike: a personality conflict.

But… could Dad have picked up on Williams family members who had a poorly-disguised dislike of Brooks? Brooks, with his sixth-grade education, was able to take good care of his wife and family all through the Great Depression. Could they have been jealous of this quietly capable man, an outsider to the family, who seemed to prosper when others failed?

Dad mentions the Mauk family and his grandmother, Annetta Mauk. Their father volunteered in the Union Army for the signing bonus, and then died far from home while convalescing from injuries received at Antietam. When their Mother remarried, the Mauk children were sent to live in an orphanage. A sad story, right?

Yes and no. We have learned that life at the Pennsylvania orphanages wasn't so bad. Pennsylvania honored their glorious dead by taking pretty good care of their orphaned children.

The three Mauk children were separated for a few years, but only because Nettie was a baby, and the babies went to a different orphanage. In time, though, the three children were reunited at one orphanage, and they all attended school until they were 16, which would have been rare for rural children at the time. We know all this from *The Civil War Soldier's Orphan Schools of Pennsylvania, 1864-1889,* and other records.

Pennsylvania's dedication to housing, feeding, clothing, and educating thousands of war orphans was unique in the nation, and touching. Though called orphanages, they operated more like private boarding schools—extensive and well-funded.

Many of the "orphans," like the Mauk children, still had a living parent, usually a Mother who was unable to provide for them.

The idea was to situate the orphans close to where they had lived. Families were encouraged to visit, and the children could be signed out and sent home for extended stays. The goal was to maintain a sense of community and connection while providing for them at a fundamental level. Those orphanages divided the day between the school room, learning practical trades, farming and housekeeping, in particular.

In the 1880 US Census, we find that Annetta, "Nettie," was living with her older brother, also named George Mauk, and his new wife Alice, in Roaring Spring. George had petitioned for Nettie to be released early, which was allowed when a family member sought it. So, our Mauk orphans had a strong family bond, which was the exact intention when the orphanages were organized and started. George, 21, was married and working at the nearby papermill. And that is where Nettie worked too.

Oddly, from the 1880 census we also know that the next door neighbors of George, Alice, and Nettie were: *Sam and Susan Myers, along with their five children!*

This leaves us to wonder exactly how estranged they all were. John Myers is listed as a laborer and he rented their small home in town. And there is his step-son, right next door, hardly more than a boy and renting the same kind of house. Could it be that Sam Myers simply had no money to send to the orphans? Family lore can be tricky. At any rate, it is here, in Roaring Spring, that Annetta met and married James Shane Williams and created their own large family.

Honey Grove Cemetery is mentioned in Dad's memoirs. This is near McCullochs Mills, another place that we Kinzer kids are familiar with. It is a lovely cemetery, full of Kinzers, Kirks, and others we're related to. It sits on a sunny hillside and generations of Dad's family are buried there.

Mom is buried there too, due to a "peculiar agreement" our parents had. Where they would be buried was a running argument between them. Dad wanted to be buried at Honey Grove, among his family. Mom was not "of" his family and she was firm about wanting to be interred in Wilmette, on the North Shore, where they had lived for decades.

It was a stalemate. So they agreed that whoever died first was truly "the loser." The surviving spouse would get to decide where they would be buried. Mom died unexpectedly at age 75, so she lost that fight and is buried among the Kinzers and their allies. If there is an afterlife, we can only imagine the "greeting" Dad got from Snippy when he finally showed up to join her.

Margaret and her kids took Dad on a road trip that included a visit to McCulloughs Mills in the summer of 2009. He directed their plans and movements, and knew all the roads as though it were 1939 and he still lived there.

They saw Vaida's marker and the rest of the family. With a little hunting they found the marker for Dr. Ritter, the doctor who treated Dad when his father, Poppy, struck him on the head with the butt of an axe on the back swing. Dr Ritter was already an old man when that happened and he died not long after. Dad also showed us where the grist mill had been when he was a boy, right where 850 crosses the creek—a cool, shady dip in the road.

When we were kids visiting his parents, Dad would say we were all going to "drive out to the country" to visit his elderly aunts and uncles who remained out that way. We always laughed at that: *how could you drive out to the country, when as far as we were concerned we were already out in the country?*

Dad loved showing off his family, and we were well-behaved kids when we understood it was important to be well-behaved. So we would put on our best manners while visiting his elderly relatives. And then we would be heathens at the Reese's where Uncle Bob would build a bonfire and Dad would buy a case of coke-colas in the old glass bottles. Despite the deposit a bottle or two would always end up in the fire so we could watch it melt.

The drive is well worth a detour if you find yourself out that way. Reeds Gap, Black Log, Honey Grove, Hollidaysburg, Chimney Rock, and Roaring Spring…it's a beautiful bit of countryside, especially in the autumn. It's a pretty drive and easy to enjoy, with lots of Kinzer-ish points of interest, and you can stop for some Ritchey's ice cream - we always found an excuse to go there on every visit.

Dad never told me about the death of James Shane Williams, but he told me about his vivid memories of the death of Will Kinzer, the day after Christmas in 1932, when Dad was eight. Neighbors had to call Brooks with the news—there was no phone at the farm house.

When Brooks, Meme and Dad arrived at the farmhouse after driving from Roaring Spring, Maggie and her friends had already washed Will's body and dressed him in his best suit. He was laid out in a simple pine coffin resting on blanks in the parlor. The curtains were drawn with an oil lamp at his head and another at his feet. The house Dad knew so well and loved, was transformed by death. Imagine a cold December day with slanting sunlight, and a body in the parlor.

The women were busy in the kitchen cooking. Meme, of course, joined the ladies. Will's three sons, Brooks, Byron, and Bivon took turns sitting with the body, a vigil that lasted two days. Dad wanted to stay in the kitchen with the women; he was just a boy after all, but Brooks, who was usually very gentle and understanding in these situations, made Jimmy sit with him.

Dad mentioned to me that he was always fascinated by the conversations women had. Women simply had better conversations in his opinion. Poppy was a quiet man. Meme was very sociable and had a large circle of friends. Family, and neighbors were in and out of their homes the whole time Dad was growing up. He mentioned that he would often come home from school to find Meme and a few friends enjoying a "pause" in their daily activities - having lemonade together on the screened porch and gossiping. Dad would sit nearby, feigning preoccupation with homework or a comic, but always sitting very quietly so he could hear more of what the women had to say.

Later, Meme became a fiend for bridge and she had a circle of girlfriends that played bridge in the mornings after the family was out the door and breakfast was cleared away. They called themselves "The Dawn Patrol."

I think Jimmy, a smart little guy, recognized the world was a complex place and he was always putting the puzzle pieces together. The gossip of women, whether playing cards or visiting, was a great source of explanations and details.

But when he was in Reeds Gap, Jimmy would be piecing the world together through his wanderings and adventures, and also through his uncles, especially Byron, a natural teacher.

His Uncles, Byron and Bivon, because they became young men at the start of the Depression, spent a few extra years at home. The early death of their father would have kept them close to their mother, too. Will's death had left Maggie Kinzer to manage the small farm on her own. The world was changing all around them and their way of life, subsistence farming, was ending. Maggie was a smart woman and she saw what was happening: the modern world. As poor as they were, she sent her children off to be trained in something that would provide a better life for them.

Besides working on the farm, Bivon managed to put together spotty employment, including at-home car repair. Dad recalled that in the summers he stayed at the farm his uncles were always repairing cars and trucks for neighbors. He recalled them methodically disassembling, cleaning and reassembling engines, axles, springs, and pumps. Apparently they could fix almost anything on wheels. Watching his uncles working together on a car, and helping them in any way he could, was a happy memory for Dad.

In his memoirs, Dad mentioned a summer when they ate a lot of ice cream in Reeds Gap. This is probably the summer of 1936, when a famous heatwave affected most of America. There was a news story about the anniversary of the heat wave, and I called Dad to ask him if he remembered it. He was abrupt with me and said he didn't remember that at all. He could be contrary that way.

But after a few minutes he called me back and said that last summer when he was 12 and visiting the farm, it was very hot. He spent a lot of that summer moving the few remaining animals from one bit of shade to another.

You milked the cows into a bucket, and then you poured that into a big canister with double walls. Usually this was enough to keep the milk sweet and fresh. But without a springhouse, and a heat wave on, the milk spoiled within hours of milking. The Dairy suspended collections. So they were using it themselves to make ice cream

He recalled that Maggie did little cooking that summer. They often ate picnic style that summer, with cold suppers on a blanket under the trees, followed by a nap.

Then he called me back again, because he realized that of course it was the heat wave of 1936, when so many temperature records were broken across America. But because they had no radio and only a local newspaper, they thought of it as just another hot summer - not a record-setting summer happening all over America.

Dad felt a deep connection to the Civil War. He told me once that when he was a boy the Civil War was all around him, even 60, 70 years later the Civil War was ever-present. Every 4th of July parade and every ceremony for Memorial Day and Veteran's Day would include an ancient uniformed Civil War vet or two. In church, his uncles pointed out the veterans, or even if you passed one on the sidewalk. It was a high honor to greet those men by name and pay your respects.

At about the time that Dad was getting serious about the Boy Scouts he was also educating himself about the Civil War. When he was 12 or 13, he began hitchhiking out to the battlefields of Gettysburg.

That he had the freedom to do this sounds incredible to our ears, but he told us many stories about tramping around the battlefield with his *U.S Army War College Guide to Gettysburg* in hand. He didn't take a tent, just a tarp and a bedroll, a rucksack of peanut butter sandwiches and apples, and nickels for fresh milk. Was Dad just as determined as his grandmother Maggie Kinzer? Were Meme and Poppy really that indulgent?

When he returned to Penn State after his service in the war, he was well on his way to graduation - the Universities were giving returning veterans credit for their service in lieu of classroom time - and heading off to law school in Washington DC. The law school he picked, George Washington, was a "workingman's college" that was focused on providing degrees and coursework for people who were already in the workforce.

I once asked Dad when his life was most in danger during his service. He said he felt he was in great danger on every mission! It was very noisy inside the plane, with engine noise and lots of motion and vibration. And while everyone was entirely focused on their assignments they were also hyper-alert to strange sounds and motions. A mission was a combination of high discipline, you had been briefed and you flew in formation, so there was a high level of routine involved in every mission. But there was also the chaos of the plane's interior and the great unknown just outside your plane. But there wasn't much time to worry about the danger you were in and maybe that was for the best.

He felt that the moments his life was *most in danger* during the war was flying over the North Atlantic on his first mission, when they hit an ice storm.

But then he thought some more and mentioned that one night of drinking in an Officer's Club in London. Dad told me the story as follows:

"Some of us had leave for London, which was a big deal. Of course, you wanted to see London! The city was a mess: we got to see exactly what the German air raids did to that city. We'd seen the news reels but to see it in person was something else.

Several of us were drinking in a very crowded officer's club: the drinks were best there and not as expensive as in a pub. English beer was hard to get used to, flat and warm, and of course they all gave you a good welcome, but then they'd charge you extra, because they knew we had the money! So we were drinking in this Officer's Club in London and over the hours we had worked our way from standing against the wall to finally sitting at a table when the buzz bombs, doodlebugs (rockets, really) started falling.

They made a loud buzzing sound that got louder and louder and then suddenly cut off. There would be silence, then a big explosion. They were designed for vengeance, and they were terrifying. Right away, I wanted to get up from the table and seek shelter. But no one else batted an eye, let alone relinquished their seat at an actual table! So I sat tight like everyone else. I really wanted to seek shelter, but no one else moved. I guess they'd been through lots worse by then. Those Londoners were stoic! It was a remarkable thing to witness."

What to make of the long passage about the Shoemans? We can only guess that Mae Shoeman was acting like a sort of babysitter for Dad, especially in those early years back in Roaring Spring. Meme was nursing her mom and dad, and then she was pregnant with JoAnn. After JoAnn's birth, Meme had several miscarriages too, due to the Rh factor. Reading between the lines, Meme may have enlisted Mae Shoeman to watch little Jimmy in order to avoid aggravation and conflicts with his grandfather, James Shane.

But what about later? Perhaps Mae Shoeman, having raised boys, just missed having a boy in her home, or maybe she had come to love Jimmy. He was certainly welcome in their house. I know that when I was about this age I was also fascinated - even a little snoopy - about the world of other families. Whatever the case, Dad was unusually involved in the Shoeman family, even after his family had moved away from Roaring Spring.

And then there is Syphilis! Why did Dad go on about syphilis at such length? I can only think it was a core memory of his life in Roaring Spring, like the poverty experienced by some of his family in the Great Depression, and the way *you* were spared. Those are troubling thoughts for a child.

At some point, we all begin to see beyond our own problems and understand the problems of others—a big step in our maturing. Jimmy had a safe, stable, comfortable life, but he was starting to see that there was a parallel reality where life wasn't so happy and cozy. Dad had a dawning realization that there was some danger lurking in the corners of the otherwise sunny and simple world of Roaring Spring.

I can also imagine that Brooks, who was watching the same sad tragedy playing out, *wanted* to talk with Jimmy about what was going on. It gave him a chance to warn his son about the pitfalls that are out there for any man, even a good one: like losing twenty dollars to a pool shark, running your car into a tree, or getting syphilis.

Dad and I were once at the Army Medical Museum in Maryland. He loved going there. They had an extensive display about sexually transmitted diseases and how the Army educated soldiers to be careful. You need healthy soldiers!

One of the displays was a model of a penis made of wax with open sores—it was very authentic looking, and extremely gross. Dad said, "They'd pass it around and it made quite an impression, I'll tell you! We'd leave that lecture swearing to remain pure. But young men will be tempted anyway."

He said he was probably one of the few soldiers who completed their tour without a single day of being unfit for duty. Time in the brig, drinking, sickness, or venereal disease were days that could be added to the back end of your service to extend your term.

Maddeningly, Dad left out some of his wonderful life stories, the ones he often told us as kids, and that's what leads me to believe that he really just wanted us to know how he had grown up, to understand where we come from. Because otherwise he could have just written a book with all the stories he told us when we were kids. He was a good storyteller, the kind who prefers to give you 120% of the truth!

For example, Jim and Snippy almost didn't get married! How he loved to tell us this one: On the morning of their wedding day he drove to Uniontown to fetch his bride and her mother, Pearl Riggs. Little did he know what awaited him. When he got there the house was in an uproar! Pearl, hurried to the curb to report that Snippy had locked her bedroom door and said she wasn't getting married after all! She'd only just graduated from college the week before and now she wasn't sure she should get married so soon. "What was the hurry? Why is everyone rushing me? Why can't I live a little as an adult on my own before I get married? What's wrong with that?" *Everything* was wrong with that, according to Pearl.

They went inside and Pearl began shouting at Snippy through the door. "You'll never get a better offer than Jimmy Kinzer!" Pearl was a striver, and she was very happy to see her third daughter marry a future lawyer.

Dad was desperate to marry Snippy and he knew right away that Pearl, with her scolding and hectoring, was only making things worse. *Mothers and daughters!* He'd seen this same sort of thing play out between his Mother and his sister JoAnn. Pearl and Snippy had to be separated. So, he asked Pearl for a sandwich and some coffee.

While she was away, he spoke quietly to Mom through the door. He figured she just had cold feet, and he was right. She was really worried about their lack of money. The magazines published these long lists of things every bride should own - sets of sheets, china, silverware, nightgowns…and she had none of those things. None of them!

Dad didn't argue. He agreed they had very little money, but that was the way all young couples started out. "Those magazines were full of bunk! You need 6 of this, you need 12 of that! Nonsense!" That's what he was thinking, but he told Snippy that one day she would have all of that and more!

And he agreed with her that they didn't have to get married that day, even though that's what he wanted. Reverse psychology? In fact, "as soon as I've finished my lunch, I'll just drive on home and tell everyone there is a delay, that's all. We can wait to get married; it isn't a problem at all."

"But gee, we''ve made some nice plans, haven't they? And I have that nice apartment in DC waiting for you. We have some big adventures ahead of us…. Wouldn't it be nice to get started on our life together?" I was desperate to marry your Mother, and here I was whistling in the dark!"

Eventually the door was unlocked, and Snippy came out in her new suit and hat. Dad pinned her corsage on, and they all drove off to Roaring Spring where they were married by Uncle Merrill in the family church. A family wedding on Memorial Day, 1949.

You can imagine the five of us kids listening to Dad tell the story, dragging it out to frighten us. Would they? Wouldn't they? It's funny that we were so anxious when our parents were right here, both of 'em - married with five children! But that's how children are, swept up in a good story, like I hope you are now.

Mom was there listening too, with one eyebrow up and her mouth firmly shut. What was she thinking while he told his version of their story? We will never know. Snippy was a bit of a sphinx that way.

Jamie was born 13 months after they married, a tiny delicate, fairy-like baby. Being new parents they were both a little anxious about hurting her, and treated her like she was made of porcelain. They had missed Maggie's funeral, due to Jamie's birth, but when she was still quite small they drove up to Roaring Spring, Altoona and Reeds Gap to show her off to Dad's extended family.

Jamie was being passed around a parlor full of elderly Kinzers and Kirks when Aunt Catherine, Dad's Great-aunt, took Jamie in her arms. Catherine started unwrapping Jamie to get a better look at her person.

"This baby is filthy!" she declared and hopped up before anyone could say anything, and carried Jamie off to her kitchen, stripping her as she went. She plopped the surprised infant in the kitchen sink and started bathing her with lye soap and a dish scrubber! Mom was horrified - that was *her baby!* But also completely intimidated by Catherine's stern conviction. You had to admire the way Catherine was holding Jamie so firmly and scrubbing away at her.

Snippy and Jim had been dabbing at Jamie with flannel washcloths, Q-tips, and the mildest baby soap! But there was Jamie, in the kitchen sink getting scrubbed hard, and cooing and laughing! "That's how you clean a baby" Aunt Clara said, handing squeaky-clean Jamie back to Mom.

Mom always laughed at this story and remarked that they soon learned how sturdy babies are, but in the first weeks they really were terrified of hurting her.

Jamie really was tiny, but also very bright-eyed, observant, and physically busy. Meme was sure that Jamie was going to take after Jimmy. He had lifted his head and shoulders at a very early date, so early that Meme took him for a studio portrait of Jimmy lying on his stomach, holding his shoulders and head high and peering at the camera man and his equipment - fully engaged with the world. A note on the photo corner noted, "Two months and seven days" to document the event. And that was Jamie too!

Dad had walked early, at nine months. Jamie lifted her head and shoulders early too, so Dad figured that Jamie (a superior baby in every way imaginable) would walk early as well.

When she was seven months old in January 1951, Dad and his law school buddy, Clyde Metzger, took charge of her on a Saturday to give Snippy a day off. They declared that besides drinking beer and listening to the boxing matches on the radio, they would get Jamie to walk!

Mom laughed at them, "She's too young to walk yet." Mom had taken child development in college and knew that babies' hips and thighs needed to reposition before babies could do more than toddle. Jamie's legs weren't there yet.

But these two men, lawyers-in-the-making, seemed to know better, and by the end of the day, Jamie *was walking* at seven months and ten days. Jamie was still a baby, though, with a large head on a small body so she looked very funny staggering along on a pair of skinny, bowed, legs. And we know the story is true, not one that was made up by Dad, because even Mom confirmed that Jamie took her first steps in the DC apartment.

A happy memory is Nature Walks with Dad. He loved taking the five of us on nature walks, often to Skokie Lagoons. He was a natural teacher and shared his love of the outdoors with us, just as his "Uncle Bairn" had. (That's how he pronounced it "Bahrn,") He'd hand out the compass, binoculars, water canteens, and the bird book; each of us had to carry something, Dad couldn't carry it all and that wouldn't be fair to him, anyway. One of his standard admonitions was, "Everyone participates in family life! That's what families are about."

He'd bring a pocket knife so we could mark our trail exactly the way the Indians did! He was wonderful that way - creating excitement from a bent branch. He could make a knapsack of baloney sandwiches, all of them made with that icky yellow mustard he loved, and apples, and a box of Hydrox cookies feel like a feast! Even the steely-tasting canteen water was a magical treat. Tap water was so cold and refreshing when drunk from a turned-up canteen.

On one hike we came across turtles sunning themselves in the spring mud. Dad decided we could each pick a turtle for a pet of our own and so we did! These were not the little turtles you could win at the fair - but great big turtles we snatched out of the mud!

We drove back to Evanston with the turtles in our laps, coming up with names for all of them as we drove along: Yertle, Myrtle, Bertyl... I don't think Snippy even let us in the door with them! She gave Dad chapter and verse about how she was NOT having five turtles in the house, and poor Dad had to put them in a box and take them straight back to Skokie Lagoons while Mom washed our hands, not with Camay, but the gritty bar of laundry soap and a nail brush! What did the turtles make of this great adventure, I wonder.

Dad was great at organizing family work parties; we were his little army of workers. "A man with five children doesn't need to pay for a lawn service, he's feeding and clothing a lawn service of his own," he would say. Maybe six times a year there would be some project he wanted us to tackle as a team - the garage, the basement, the yard. On Friday night he would warn us that there would be all hands on deck first thing on Saturday morning. No shirkers and no lollygagging in front of the TV!

He'd make pancakes for us while he explained what we'd be doing that day, and *why we were doing it* - so important for children. Then he'd lay out exactly what was expected of us.

Taking the storm windows down and putting up the screens is a great example. He'd say, "We do this so we can open our windows and have some fresh air. Won't that be nice after a long winter all closed up?" And then he'd break it down into all the tasks to achieve that goal and assign them to us based on capability and strength.

The boys and Dad got to use the ladder and hand things up and down, but the twins had a fun assignment too. We got to use the stiff wire brush! It was our job to brush down the screens (BOTH sides) before they went up the ladder! Jamie was in charge of hosing off the windows - commanding the hose was a very responsible assignment! When the screens were all up, and the windows hosed down, we were ready to stack them in the garage rafters, passing them up to Dad in a special order.

Dirty and hungry, there'd be tomato soup and grilled cheezers in the kitchen and a de-briefing on the morning's activities. Dad relished those days and so did we. He took something onerous and made it seem like a grand accomplishment instead. We were contributors, participants, *and members of the Kinzer family!* And those were all great things to be.

Dad was a very natural father, and I think his memoirs show that there is a strong genetic component to fathering: Will, though living the hard life of a farmer, was a good father to his children. Brooks and Uncle Byron inherited that and so did Jimmy. I can't help but notice that both of my brothers were very comfortable in the role of "Dad" and I'm guessing all five of my nephews will be good fathers, too. Genetics or modeling - I don't know, but it is generational.

Dad was a hard worker himself and goal oriented. And he was gentle in his corrections and guidance. He liked us to be spirited and independent, and he didn't want to squash us the way he had seen James Shane Williams do to his family - ordering them around and correcting them with his cane.

When our brother John Byron was a Junior in college he was spending a long dry season living at home while taking classes and working full time. He was also preparing for the MCATs, another full time job. He was having NO FUN and was starting to resent it.

After dinner one night, Dad took Barney out in the back yard to sit and have a beer together. At first it was Dad's usual musings: "I have the best family," "No Father could be prouder," "Ain't life grand?"

But slowly the conversation switched to Barney's goal to be a doctor and what a bad year he was having. John said he was missing the good times with his friends, baseball and hanging out. His spirits were flagging.

Dad simply pointed out that the one, a summer of no fun, was necessary for the other, becoming a Doctor. "Barney, four years from now we can be sitting out here having a beer together and talking about you playing ball and drinking with your buddies, while you load trucks for a living...or we could be sitting here and talking about you completing medical school. It's as simple as that. The next four years will pass by no matter which path you choose. Why not choose the path that leads to a better future?" Dad was a successful lawyer but what he really excelled at was fathering.

One of my fondest memories of Dad is sitting outside with him as the night closed in. He'd invite you to step outside with him after dinner at 2409 Lawndale. He'd set up a couple of folding chairs, mix himself a martini, and settle in for some stargazing. He might start by pointing out the constellations and important stars above, and then telling you how he would sit out like this in the evening with his grandparents, dad, and uncles, winding down after a long day on the farm. With the night sky of rural Pennsylvania he could see twice the stars were seeing.

Eventually he always came around to his favorite topic: how lucky we were to be Kinzers, what a great family to be a part of, how nice it was to have each other, and how proud he was of us.

Dad died in 2016. He left this earth with great reluctance. Fate had been kind to him and he hoped to be the first Kinzer to see 100.

How he would have enjoyed witnessing his ever-expanding family: four weddings, bringing four new faces to our family, two new grandsons and two new granddaughters, and, hopefully, more on the way. The two great-granddaughters he knew are now becoming accomplished young women, and his own children have transitioned to being grandparents and retirees. He would have found it all quite marvelous.

Dad was a good one for bucking you up. If you were down about something that hadn't gone your way he would remind you that "...the littlest birds sing in a storm, have you noticed that? They do it to keep their courage up!"

He was inclined towards happiness, even so his heart was big enough to hold the sadder parts of life too. The Kinzers are lucky people, but they were never free of tragedy. I'm thinking of the deaths of infant Theodore and the passing of my brother Jim. Dad really poured himself into his boys, and those losses would have weighed on him. Dad was a witness to the truth that: terrible things can happen to you and you have to learn to accept it. War, disease, poverty, bad luck and fate. Perhaps a memoir like this one, with so many happy and sad tales in it, helps to place our personal stories within the larger story of our family and then within our three centuries in America.

www.ingramcontent.com/pod-product-compliance
Lightning Source LLC
Chambersburg PA
CBHW040903120626
46551CB00006B/625